Reaching Up
for
Manhood

ALSO BY GEOFFREY CANADA

Fist Stick Knife Gun:
*A Personal History of Violence
in America*

Reaching Up
for
Manhood

....

Transforming the Lives
of Boys in America

....

Geoffrey Canada

BEACON PRESS
BOSTON

Beacon Press
25 Beacon Street
Boston, Massachusetts 02108-2892
http://www.beacon.org

Beacon Press books are published
under the auspices of the
Unitarian Universalist Association of Congregations.

11 10 09 08 07   13 12 11 10 9

Book design by Boskydell Studio
Composition by Wilsted & Taylor Publishing Services

Library of Congress Cataloging-in-Publication Data

Canada, Geoffrey.
Reaching up for manhood : transforming the lives
of boys in America / Geoffrey Canada.
p. cm.
ISBN 978-0-8070-2317-4 (paper)
1. Boys—United States—Psychology.   2. Boys—United States—Social
conditions.   3. Afro-American boys—Psychology.   4. Afro-American boys
—Social conditions.   5. Masculinity—United States.   I. Title.
HQ775.C35   1998
305.23—DC21   97-19919

To my children:

*Those named—Melina, Jerry, Bruce,
Pascal, Alex, Sandra, Regine, Elsie, Humberto,
and Raymond—and those not named.*

I love you. Don't forget it.

Contents

Preface

THEY WERE dying again. There was no one I could talk to—I felt I was the only one who could see the connection, that my friends from two different places of my growing up, the South Bronx and Wyandanch, Long Island, were dying. It brought on the feeling that it would never end, that my men friends would die and die, and keep on dying until I would be the only man left at the funeral. I knew I was overreacting, but this was not the first time death had run up the score on me, had taken my friends, not one every now and then, but in bunches.

Most of the deaths happened a long time ago, when we were young men. Back then the calls came one after another, bringing the news of another friend lost. It got so that after the first sentence you knew what was to follow.

"Geoff, has anybody told you? It's D. J., man. He's dead."

"You heard about Mikey? Aw man, he just had a kid. OD'd."

"You ain't gonna believe this. They found Warren in a lot with trash and stuff. They killed him."

"I don't know what it was. They said he just died. Was sick or something."

And then, just like that, it stopped. And those of us who survived and became men, and started families, remembered our friends. We thought about why so many died so young. We retold stories about how recklessly we'd lived life in our youth. For all of us it started when we were boys. We were raised on old myths and tall tales of what it meant to be a boy, and what it took to become a man. We were taught to love being tough. We played contact sports and laughed in glee at opponents knocked senseless on the football field, and for these small bits of viciousness we were pounded on the back, or patted on the backside—the ultimate one-hundred-percent-all-male thing you could do in a sporting environment. We learned to do all the things that we were taught men did; we played hard and fought hard, drank hard and drugged hard. And in the end those of us left could look back and see we'd paid the price.

But the deaths had stopped many years ago, and in my forties I'd become convinced that I would be able to grow old with my friends, the boys who had survived to become men. Now suddenly death was back.

Frank was first. I'd gone to high school with him in Wyandanch. He was best friends with my younger brother, Reuben, and had spent many a day and night with us when we were kids. He was forty-three.

I was still reeling from the news of Frank's death when I heard about Clarence. Clarence had the apartment underneath my family's when we lived on Union Avenue in the South Bronx. When my brothers and I wrestled and jumped off our beds, it was Clarence's family that complained about the noise and the plaster falling from the ceiling. Clarence died at forty-five.

Eddie died the same week. We were family through marriage. My brother John married Eddie's cousin Dorothy. We all played varsity football and basketball together. When that call came in I kept asking over and over, "You mean *Eddie*? Eddie who I played basketball and football with? *That* Eddie?" Eddie died at the age of forty-five.

Three deaths in two weeks. For a while I was afraid to hear the telephone ring, fearing it would be more bad news. The deaths had reminded me and my remaining friends from high school that we were quickly becoming the last of our group. At the funerals you couldn't help but notice that there were many women from high school and few men. I was also struck by the fact that both Eddie and Frank had sons who were young men now as we had been. I was drawn to them, imagining how deep their grief must be over losing their fathers. I imagined how my own sons would feel and wanted to say something to ease their pain. I pulled each one of the boys over and told them what good men their fathers had been. I talked about how kind and generous they were, how much love they had in their hearts. I told them about their sense of loyalty and fair play, the fact that they would do anything to help a friend in need. I told the sons that their fathers were strong men, proud men, compassionate men.

Later, after the shock of the deaths had begun to wear off and I was convinced that the Grim Reaper had found greener pastures to harvest for a while, I reflected on what I had said to Frank and Eddie's sons about their fathers. I realized I hadn't told them that both of their fathers were tough, could fight with the best of them, had what we used to call heart. I hadn't told Eddie's son about the time I got lost and went into a bar to ask directions and got chased away because they didn't allow blacks in that bar. How Eddie was so furious he made us go back and dared anyone to "ever mess with my cousin again." How single-handedly he had cowed the whole bar. Now *that* was heart. These were the kinds of actions that we thought defined manhood when we were young, yet I had told the sons about their fathers' softer sides, about the things we would never admit to being or feeling when we were teenagers.

The deaths of these three friends in such quick succession brought home a lesson I'd begun to learn six or seven years before. In my old neighborhood in the South Bronx, the first Sunday in August is called Old Timers' Day. On that day each year, those of us who grew up in the area come to a local playground where as children we played basketball and softball, and we talk and reminisce about the old days on the block. At first when I began going to Old Timers' Day I would search out people I hadn't seen in thirty years and try to associate these men with the children I had run the streets with. And I was so happy to see that some of us had made it that it took me three or four Old Timers' Day celebrations before I began to notice that many of my friends, these men I thought were so lucky to have survived those tough years growing up, had actually developed habits as boys that they continued as men, and that they were far down the road to self-destruction.

It got so that each year we stood around and talked about who had died the year before. So many of the deaths involved alcohol and cigarettes. As boys we were hard-drinking, two-packs-a-day cigarette-smoking teenagers, and proud of it. After college, I had stopped the smoking and the heavy drinking, although many of my friends had not, and I still thought that if you lived to be an adult without being hooked on hard drugs you had made it. Now I was shocked to see what two or three decades of excessive use of alcohol and tobacco could do to someone. These men looked old beyond their years. Looking at my friends, I began to realize that the things we did as young boys were still haunting many of us as we entered our forties.

More and more I have become concerned with what boys think they should be, with what they believe it means to be a man. Our beliefs about maleness, the mythology that surrounds being male, has led many boys to ruin. The image of male as strong is mixed with the image of male as violent. Male as virile gets confused with male as promiscuous. Male as adventurous equals male as reckless. Male as intelligent often gets mixed with male as arrogant, racist, and sexist. If we look around and see too many men in jail, on drugs, abandoning their families, acting without compassion or even violently, we as a society must shoulder the blame and take responsibility for change. Boys find themselves pulled and tugged by forces beyond their control as they make the confusing and sometimes perilous trip to manhood. Some lose their way. While reaching up for manhood they tumble over a moral and ethical precipice and many can never scale their way back up. We must all spend more time trying to understand what happens to boys—and how we can help shape them into better men.

And to do this we must acknowledge that we face a crisis. I am concerned that there is a false sense of security in our country about how our boys are faring. In recent years, as we have acknowledged that our girls are in trouble and have mobilized to try to help them (the best-known research has concentrated on girls' schooling), we have assumed that boys, on average, experience fewer gender-specific stresses. This is wrong. More than 1,300,000 arrests of boys under the age of eighteen were made in 1995 (Federal Bureau of Investigation, Uniform Crime Reporting Program, table 33). *The Real War on Crime* (1996, edited by Stephen R. Donziger) points out the alarming fact that at least one of every four males in America has an arrest record. And for those who think boys are doing well in school, recent evidence suggests otherwise: a 1997 *Boston Globe* article notes that "several new studies highlight the problems boys have in reading and writing, showing that they are far worse than the well-advertised problems for girls in math and science" (Kate Zernike, "Focusing on Boys," 6 January 1997).

The problems facing black boys are even more debilitating. As a percentage of boys in America, they are killed more often by violence, they are arrested more frequently; they are dropping out of school, not going on to college, and not being fathers to their children in record numbers. And there is new evidence to suggest that the situation of the poorest of black boys continues to take a heavy toll even into adulthood. Bob Herbert reports in the *New York Times*, "Two-thirds of the boys who reach the age of 15 in Harlem can expect to die in young or mid-adulthood—that is, before they reach the age of 65. Fifteen-year-old boys in Harlem have less chance of surviving even to 45 than their white counterparts nationwide have of reaching 65" (2 December 1996, p. A15).

Even given these alarming facts, why a book solely on boys? I know from personal experience that girls in America are facing similar perils. They are with increasing frequency joining gangs, using drugs, having unsafe sex, and acting violently. Their numbers are increasing in our juvenile detention facilities. This book is not an attempt to magnify the crisis facing boys so that it diminishes the spotlight on girls. Instead I hope to illustrate how our children are shaped by the complex cultural context in which they grow up, and to show that gender has more impact on the ways our children are exposed to and handle risk and stress than I think we have acknowledged. Even when boys and girls end up at the same place in terms of being in trouble, they get there by different routes. Part of the answer in how we help them is to understand the routes they have traveled so that we can find ways to guide them from the road leading to ruin and destruction to the ones leading to success and salvation.

Healing

I T WAS THE spring of 1984 and I had been director of Rheedlen's afterschool program for two years. It was a typical afternoon—children were playing board games, some were drawing, all seemed settled and happy. I decided that I wanted to watch the boys playing touch football outside on the playground. They were all between ten and twelve, the age when yelling and screaming while you run as fast as you can is more fun than you ever dreamed. Bobbie was fast, and he surprised the other boys by darting left, then right. He was wide open, and the ball well thrown, which was a surprise to everyone since the eleven-year-old quarterback hadn't managed a good throw at all up until that moment. Bobbie and the ball were destined to meet at the same place at the same time. The catch was flawless. Why he then tripped and fell nobody could see.

I was thirty feet away when he went down and could tell immediately that something was wrong. Bobbie started to get up, looked at his leg, and flopped back to the ground screaming. Later we figured he must have fallen on a piece of glass. I ran to him as fast as I could. I could tell by the way the boys who'd reached Bobbie first now just stood back from him and stared that they knew this injury was a more serious one than they could handle. Bobbie had on short pants, and I could see the cut on his calf was a bad one. The leg was bleeding freely, and I was sure that to the other boys it looked as if blood was everywhere, but I could tell no major blood vessels were cut. I yelled to one of the staff to call an ambulance.

Bobbie was badly frightened and looked as if he was about to go into shock. I knew I had to calm him down. I talked softly to him. Told him that he was going to be all right. I explained that he was going to have to get stitches but that he would probably be back at our program in a day or two. Bobbie was crying and asking for his mother. I gently stroked his hand as I talked to him, letting him know his mother would meet him at the hospital. I feel that up until that point I did a good job of handling the situation. It was what happened next that I have worried about for many years.

The ambulance took about ten minutes to get to the playground. I had managed to get Bobbie calmed down by the time it arrived. As I saw the attendants coming with a stretcher, I wiped the tears away from Bobbie's eyes with some napkins that had been brought to me.

"You did real good, Bobbie. I'm proud of you. Now, I don't want you to be scared. I'm going to send Sam with you to the hospital. The doctor is probably going to have to give you a few stitches, like I said. I want you to be a big boy and not be scared, okay?"

"Okay," he said as tears began to fall from his eyes again.

"I want you to tell me all about what happens when you come back to Rheedlen, okay?"

"Okay," he answered as they loaded him in the back of the ambulance. Sam, one of our social work staff, sat on the seat next to him. As they closed the door I waved and Bobbie waved back. He tried to look brave, like a big boy. I was so proud of him.

Just as I'd predicted, Bobbie was back at Rheedlen the next day. He had a brand-new bandage covering the ten stitches it had taken to close the cut on his leg. The first thing Bobbie did when he saw me was to declare so all could hear, "Geoff, I got ten stitches and I didn't even cry."

"What?" I said. "You mean you didn't cry at all?"

"Nope. I didn't cry at all."

"I don't believe you," I said, allowing him to enjoy his moment of triumph.

"If you don't believe me, you can ask my mother. She was right there. She'll tell you. I didn't cry the whole time."

"Wow! You're becoming quite a young man. Ten stitches. No tears. I'm proud of you."

And for the rest of the afternoon Bobbie told all who would listen how he had not cried when his leg was being stitched up. And the responses he received from the adults were all the same. We were proud of him. We slapped him five, we shook his hand, we admired his courage. And other little boys began to tell me how they had cut their hands, or heads, or broken their arms or legs, and they hadn't cried either. And I heaped praise on them and told them what big boys they were and how proud I was of them.

There are lots of things I would do differently today. I would say to Bobbie, "It's all right to cry. Men cry all the time. If the stitches hurt and you cry, that's normal." After he came back to the program I'd spend time with him, helping him deal with his injury, trying to see if the scar on the outside had created a scar on the inside. I would tell him I don't think it's right that boys are rarely taught to talk about the hurt on the outside, and almost never to talk about the pain on the inside. I'd tell him it's not always good to just pick yourself up, brush yourself off, and not make a big deal out of it.

The point I am trying to make about how boys are taught to deal with injury is underlined beautifully by a scene in the first *Jaws* movie. Hooper, the movie's hero, is on the boat with the captain, who has no use for this college-educated intellectual, a man not as tough and hard as he and his crew. It is nighttime and the two are drinking, on their way to getting drunk. They begin to compare scars, scars caused by encounters with things that bite in the ocean. With each scar revealed, their mutual respect grows. As they are rolling up shirtsleeves and pulling up pants legs, pointing out old wounds with pride and hinting at the underlying trauma associated with each one, finally the tough, callous captain is asked about his biggest scar. And because of the drinking and his newfound respect for Hooper, he tells of the never-to-be-forgotten horror of being in the water with others, watching his friends being killed by sharks. As he opens up and tells of his pain, we realize that all these years he has been keeping that pain and hurt bottled up inside him. As the tough exterior of his maleness cracks and we see his vulnerability, we wonder how he will ever be able to recover and become the uncaring, tough-as-nails sea captain he has been. Of course the giant shark attacks just then and saves him from his quick foray into vulnerability. He instantly reverts back to his old self and stays that way even as he is being eaten by his worst nightmare.

Boys are taught to suffer their wounds in silence. To pretend that it doesn't hurt, outside or inside. So many of them carry the scars of childhood into adulthood, never having come to grips with the pain, the anger, the fear. And that pain can change boys and bring doubts into their lives, though more often than not they have no idea where those doubts come from. Pain can make you afraid to love or cause you to doubt the safety of the ground you walk on. I know from my own experience that some pain changes us forever.

It all started because there was no grass. Actually, there was grass, you just couldn't walk on it.

In the late fifties and early sixties, the projects were places people moved to get away from tenement buildings like mine. We couldn't move into the projects because my mother was a single parent. Today most projects are crammed full of single parents, but when I was a child your application for the projects was automatically rejected if that was your situation. The projects were places for people on the way up. They had elevators, they were well maintained, and they had grass surrounding them. Grass like we had never seen before. The kind of grass that was like walking on a carpet. Grass that yelled out to little boys and girls to run and tumble and do cartwheels and roll around on it. There was just one problem, it was off limits to people. All the projects had signs that said "Keep Off the Grass." And there were men keeping their eyes open for children who dared even think of crossing the single-link chain that enclosed it. The projects didn't literally have the *only* grass we could find in the Bronx. Crotona Park, Pelam Bay Park, and Van Courtland Park were available to us. But the grass in those parks was a sparse covering for dirt, rocks, and twigs. You would never think about rolling around in that grass, because if you did you'd likely be rolling in dog excrement or over a sharp rock.

There was one other place where we found grass in our neighborhood. Real grass. Lawn-like grass. It was in the side yard of a small church that was on the corner of Union Avenue and Home Street. The church was small and only open on Sundays. The yard and its precious grass were enclosed by a four-foot-high fence. We were not allowed in the yard by the pastor of the church. Occasionally we would sneak in to retrieve a small pink Spalding ball that had gone off course during a game of stickball or punch ball, but if we were seen climbing the fence there would be a scene, with screams, yells, and threats to tell our parents. So although we often looked at that soft grass with longing, the churchyard was off limits.

It would have stayed off limits if it had not been for football. Football came into my life one fall when I was nine years old, and I played it every fall for the rest of my childhood and adolescence. But football in the inner city looked very different from football played in other places. The sewer manhole covers were the end zones. Anywhere in the street was legal playing territory, but not the sidewalk. There could be no tackling on pavement, so the game was called two-hand touch. If you touched an opponent with both hands, play had to stop. The quarterback called colorful plays: "Okay now. David, you go right in front of the blue Chevy. I'm gonna fake it to you. Geoff, see the black Ford on the right? No, don't look, stupid—they're gonna know our play. You go there, stop, then cross over toward William's stoop. I'll look for you short. Richard, go to the first sewer and turn around and stop. I'll pump it to you, go long. Geoff, you hike on three. Ready! Break!"

We knew how real football was played because we all watched the New York Giants every Sunday. We simply didn't have the equipment or the field to play tackle football. That changed when I was ten years old and received for Christmas a pair of shoulder pads and a helmet. The equipment was cheap and provided barely any protection, but when I put it on I looked, I was sure, absolutely fearsome. Several other boys received football equipment that Christmas as well, and so there we were on the street feeling like "real" football players. No one had cleats, or pants with knee pads, thigh pads, and a padded girdle, or elbow pads, or mouthpieces. But with a helmet and maybe shoulder pads, we were ready to block, tackle, and run for glory. All we needed was grass. All our eyes were drawn to the churchyard. A decision had to be made. Rory was the first to bring it up. "We should sneak into the churchyard and play tackle."

I acted as the voice of reason. "What if we get caught? The preacher said he would tell our mothers."

"Whatssamatta, Geoff? You scared? So what if he tells? He don't even know our mothers."

"Well, what if he calls the police? What if they take us to jail? If I go to jail my mother's gonna beat me. I don't want to get no beating."

"He's not gonna call no police. Even if he do, the police can't lock you up just for being in a yard. Can they?" Here we were all on shaky ground. The police did whatever they wanted to do in our eyes. We didn't know what they might do.

Tommy gave us the answer. "Look, if the preacher comes out—right?—we'll all run to the back of the fence and climb over. Then we run up Home Street so he thinks that we live up there. He won't be able to see our faces and he won't know where we live."

With the matter of going to jail settled and no threat that we might end up having to answer to our parents, we all walked over to Home Street and, out of sight of front windows, climbed over the fence and walked onto the grass. A thick carpet of grass that felt like falling on a mattress. We were in heaven.

Football in the churchyard was everything we had imagined. We could finally block and tackle and not worry about falling on the hard concrete or asphalt streets. We didn't have to worry about cars coming down the block the way we did when we played two-hand touch. And because we were able to tackle, we could have running plays. We loved it. We played for hours on end.

Sneaking into the churchyard became a regular part of our play activity. Many weekends or afternoons we couldn't play there because we could see someone was in the church, but if we thought it was empty, over the fence we climbed and the game would begin. Sometimes, unbeknownst to us, the preacher would be home, and out he would come yelling and saying he was going to tell our parents. We'd scramble over the back fence like boot camp trainees who have mastered the obstacle course. The excitement and fear made us giddy. We would run up Home Street and come back to Union Avenue via a network of connecting alleyways, ending up on a stoop far away from the church, out of breath and laughing at how slow Alan ran because he was fat, or at the look of panic in Greg's eyes when his shirt got caught on the top of the fence and he thought the preacher was going to catch him. We would laugh and tease and boast about who would have won the game if we had finished it, and we would start planning the next opportunity to sneak in.

There was one problem with our football field, which was about thirty yards long and fifteen yards wide: at the far end there was a built-in barbecue pit, right in the middle of the end zone. If we were running with the football, or going out for a pass, we had to avoid the barbecue pit with its metal rods along the top, set into its concrete sides. We knew that no matter what you were doing when in that area of the yard, you had to keep one eye on the barbecue pit. To run into its concrete sides—or, even worse, the metal bars—would be very painful and dangerous.

I was fast and crafty. I loved to play split end on the offense. I could fake out the other kids and get free to catch the ball. I had one problem, though—I hadn't mastered catching a football thrown over my head. To do this you have to lean your head back and watch as the football descends into your hands. Keep your eye on the ball, that's the trick to catching one over the shoulder.

We all wanted to go deep for "the bomb"—a ball thrown as far as possible, where a receiver's job is to run full speed and catch it with outstretched hands. It took me forever to learn to concentrate on the football, with my head back as far as it would go, while running full speed. But finally I mastered it. I was now a truly dangerous receiver. If you played too far away from me I could catch the ball short, and if you came too close I could run right by the slower boys and catch the bomb.

The move I did on Ned was picture perfect. I ran ten yards, turned around, and faced Walter. He pumped the ball to me. I felt Ned take a step forward, going for the fake as I turned and ran right by him. Walter launched the bomb. As the football left his hand I stopped looking over my shoulder at him and started my sprint to the end zone. After running ten yards I tilted my head back and looked up at the bright blue fall sky. Nothing. I looked forward again and ran harder, then looked up again. There it was, the brown leather football falling in a perfect arc toward the earth, toward where I would be in three seconds, toward the winning touchdown.

And then pain. The bar of the barbecue pit caught me in midstride in the middle of my shin. I went down in a flurry of ashes, legs and arms flying every which way. The pain was all-enveloping. I grabbed my leg above and below where it had hit; I couldn't bear to touch the place where it had slammed into the bar. The pain was too much. I lay flat on the ground, trying to cry out. I could only make a humming sound deep in the back of my throat. My friends gathered around and I tried to act like a big boy, the way I had been taught. I tried not to cry. Then the pain consumed me and I couldn't see any of my friends anymore. I howled and then cried and then howled some more. The boys saw the blood seeping through my dungarees and my brother John said, "Let me see. Be still. Let me see." He rolled my pants leg up to my knee to look at the damage. All the other boys who had been playing or watching were in a circle around me. They all grimaced and turned away. I knew it was bad then, and I howled louder.

Catching the metal bar in full stride with my shin had crushed a quarter-size hole in my leg. The skin was missing and even to this day I can feel the indentation in my shinbone where the bar gouged out a small piece of bone. I was off my feet for a few days and it took about two weeks for my shin to heal completely. Still, I was at the age where sports and friends meant everything to me. I couldn't wait to play football in the churchyard again, but I was a much more cautious receiver than before.

Several years later, when I finished the ninth grade at a junior high school in the South Bronx and was preparing to go to high school, I knew that my life had reached a critical juncture. My high school prospects were grim. I didn't pass the test to get into the Bronx High School of Science (I was more interested in girls than prep work), so my choices were either Morris High School or Clinton High School. Both of these were poor academically and suffered from a high incidence of violence. I asked my mother if I could stay with my grandparents in the house they had just built in Wyandanch, a quiet, mostly African-American town on Long Island. She agreed and they agreed, so I went there for my three years of high school.

That first year I went out for the junior varsity football team at Wyandanch High and played football as a receiver. I was a good receiver. The years of faking out kids on the narrow streets of the Bronx made me so deceptive that I couldn't be covered in the wide-open area of a real football field. But I had one problem—I couldn't catch the bomb. My coach would scream at me after the ball had slipped through my fingers or bounced off my hands. "Geoff! What's the matter with you? Concentrate, goddamn it!

Concentrate!" I couldn't. No matter how I tried to focus on the ball coming down out of the sky, at the last minute I would have to look down. To make sure the ground wasn't playing tricks on me. No hidden booby traps. What happened in the churchyard would flash into my mind and even though I knew I was in a wide-open field, I'd have to glance down at the ground. I never made it as a receiver in high school. I finished my career as quarterback. Better to be looking at your opponent, knowing he wanted to tackle you, sometimes even getting hit without seeing it coming, but at least being aware of that possibility. Never again falling into the trap of thinking you were safe, running free, only you and the sky and a brown leather ball dropping from it.

Boys are conditioned not to let on that it hurts, never to say, "I'm still scared." In this chapter I've written only about physical trauma, but every day in my work I deal with boys undergoing almost unthinkable mental trauma from violence or drug abuse in the home, or carrying emotional scars from physical abuse or unloving parents. I have come to see that in teaching boys to deny their own pain we inadvertently teach them to deny the pain of others. I believe this is one of the reasons so many men become physically abusive to those they supposedly love. Pain suffered early in life often becomes the wellspring from which rage and anger flow, emotions that can come flooding over the banks of restraint and reason, often drowning those unlucky enough to get caught in their way. We have done our boys an injustice by not helping them to acknowledge their pain. We must remember to tell them "I know it hurts. Come let me hold you. I'll hold you until it stops. And if you find out that the hurt comes back, I'll hold you again. I'll hold you until you're healed."

Boys are taught by coaches to play with pain. They are told by parents that they shouldn't cry. They watch their heroes on the big screen getting punched and kicked and shot, and while these heroes might groan or yell, they never cry. And even some of us who should know better don't go out of our way to make sure our boys know about our own pain and tears, and how we have healed ourselves. By sharing this we can give boys models for their own healing and recovery.

Even after I was grown I believed that ignoring pain was part of learning to be a man, that I could get over hurt by simply willing it away. I had forgotten that when I was young I couldn't run in an open field without looking down, that with no one to talk to me about healing, I spent too many years unable to trust the ground beneath my feet.

Risk

I'D ARRIVED at work at Rheedlen as usual at eight-fifteen. When I was handed a telephone message that Roland had called at seven-thirty that morning, my eyebrows raised. Roland was one of the boys I'd taught in my martial arts class for years, and I considered him a son. He wouldn't be calling that early unless something was wrong. But his message said I couldn't reach him. So, worried as I was, there was nothing I could do about it but start on my round of morning meetings. One of them took me across town, and I got back to Rheedlen at around two-thirty in the afternoon. I had just started dialing the first number from my accumulated messages when from my intercom I heard the announcement that Roland was on line four. I quickly took the call.

"How you doing, Roland? I heard you tried to call me this morning."

"I'm doing okay. Well, I'm not really doing okay because I'm already late for work and they won't let me go."

"Who won't let you go?"

"The police."

My heart began to beat a little faster. "You've been arrested?"

"No, they're just holding me for questioning."

"Questioning about what?" I asked, feeling slightly relieved.

"About a murder." My heart sank. My God, I thought, not murder. "They have me and Analdo and Scottie," Roland added.

"They have you for murder? They think you killed somebody?"

"No, no. They don't think we murdered somebody—we were witnesses. They've been holding us since three-thirty last night. I told them I had to go to work, but they just keep saying we can't leave, we have to stay."

"Is the person in charge of the investigation there with you now?" I asked.

"Yeah. He's standing right here."

"Let me speak to him." In a few seconds a very professional police investigator was on the phone. I told him who I was, that I could vouch for Roland and for the other young men, and that the police could always reach them through Rheedlen. I explained that they had jobs they had to get to, and I would appreciate it if they could be interviewed right away and released. The officer said he would see what he could do and I asked that he put Roland back on the phone.

"Roland, listen—when you guys are released I want you to come see me at my office."

"All right," he answered and hung up the phone.

I breathed a sigh of relief, feeling better now that I knew the three were not accused of murder. I knew these boys, and they were no murderers. But if you're poor, and black or Latino, and are in any way linked to a serious crime, you are almost always presumed guilty. I had already begun to imagine the nightmare of jail, and trying to raise money for bail, and trying to find a good lawyer. So thank God they were not accused of murder. But there was still a problem. They might have witnessed a killing. And, being young men, they would try to make believe it was no big deal. They would never admit how scared they were, or seek counseling to help deal with the trauma of being that close to death. They would try to do what all my boys try to do—laugh it off, say "Better him than me."

I sat at my desk and wondered about this new scar that would be etched on my boys' lives. I had known two of the three since they were children. They were part of an original group who began in my martial arts class back in the mid-eighties. There are eight of them, five boys and three girls who have been with me for over a decade. We have stuck with each other through thick and thin, and over the years I have watched them grow up to be fine young men and women, and they know I love them as I love my own children. Most of them have grown up without a father in their lives, and in private and in public I refer to them as my sons and daughters. And while both my boys and my girls have had their own sets of problems, it was the boys that always seemed to teeter on the brink of disaster. Even as they got older I knew that they were still at great risk. So I waited for my boys and their friend to come in and to tell me about the murder.

The three of them arrived about two hours later and I had them come to my office right away. They hadn't been to sleep at all but I could tell that the adrenaline from the night's events had them still wide awake. I asked Roland what had happened.

"We went to this club in Brooklyn. It's like a reggae club. Analdo works there as a bouncer. I worked there as a bouncer a few times but I stopped. Me and Scottie was over by the speakers listening to the music. Analdo was at the front door with the other security, searching people for weapons. We was just hanging out in the club when we heard this loud gunshot. Everybody stopped dancing and started running."

"Where were you in relation to the shooting?" I asked.

"That's the crazy part. He shot the guy right next to me. I mean I was right here and they killed the guy not three feet from me," Roland said, shaking his head.

"Did you see the guy get shot?" I asked.

"Naw, I wasn't looking. By the time I heard the shot and turned, the guy was already on the floor. He was just lying there and you could see all of this blood coming out of his head."

"What did you do then? Did you see the guy that shot him?"

"No. When I saw the guy on the floor, me and Scottie ran the other way. Everybody was running. We dived on the floor and people kept piling on top of us. We were happy to be on the bottom. That way if the guy kept shooting we'd have everyone on top, for protection."

"Then what happened?" I asked.

"After a few minutes everybody got up and started looking at the guy who was shot. He was still alive, but they shot him in the head. You could see the blood just pouring out of his head. He kept asking for help. He said, 'Don't let me die. Don't let me die.' We didn't know what to do. Then he just stopped talking. Then he just died."

"Were you scared?" I asked.

Scottie, the youngest of the three, answered first. "I don't know about Roland and Analdo, but when I heard that gunshot I panicked."

"I was at the door when I heard what I thought was a gunshot," Analdo said. "At first I didn't know what it was, then suddenly all these people came running out of the club. I tried to get in to see what was happening, but I couldn't fight my way through the people running out."

"I don't think that was too smart," I said. "The last thing you want to do is confront a person who just killed somebody. You should have stayed where you were and called the police."

"Well, I knew Roland and Scottie were inside. I just wasn't thinking. I wanted to make sure they were all right," Analdo responded.

"What about you, Roland?"

"When I heard the shot, I wasn't scared at first. I just acted from reflex. I remember you told us if people are shooting, hit the ground. I turned and looked and then I thought, 'What are you looking for? You ought to be getting on the floor.' But you know it was kind of like *not real*. Like a dream or something. Then when I saw the guy on the floor bleeding, I said this ain't no dream. And I dived for cover. Then after it was all over and I was thinking that guy on the floor could have been me, then I got scared."

"It's all right to be scared," I said. "I would have been scared. Anybody with good sense would have been scared in that situation. I'm glad you guys are all right. Go home and get some sleep, then come back and see me—we should talk. I don't think it's such a good idea for you to be going to clubs where people end up getting killed. And Analdo, I think your career as a bouncer should come to an end."

After the boys left I wasn't convinced that they would heed my warnings once the shock of their close encounter with death had worn off. I thought about how so many boys continuously get involved in situations that most of us would consider too dangerous, too risky. I am convinced that boys are pushed early in their lives to be risk takers. That they see situations that contain a certain element of danger as a challenge they must continuously confront. And they deny the one thing that allows most of us to evaluate when a situation is too risky—fear. There are five words that have gotten more boys into trouble than anything else I know: "What's the matter—you scared?"

Boys are taught by their peers, and often by their parents, that fear must be denied, never admitted. And as they meet and overcome these small challenges as boys, they find that their identity, their self-worth becomes tied to this risk-taking behavior. My friends and I were so accustomed to taking risks when we were young that we didn't even consider what we were doing as being risky. Indeed, risk taking became such a part of our lives that we were bored with activities that didn't offer some element of risk. So simply going to a party was not nearly as much fun as going to a party where there might be trouble.

The problem is that once a boy is invested in his reputation for not being scared to take risks, where does he draw the line? And when once the most risky thing boys might do was drive a car a hundred miles an hour, today, with the proliferation of handguns among young people, and the fact of AIDS, and the new potency of heroin, for instance, risk-taking behavior has become more deadly. Because so many have been killed by guns, you can begin to see a not-so-subtle change in how boys feel about risk-taking behavior. Where they once took risks because they felt invincible, because they couldn't imagine anything could happen to them, today you find more and more boys who truly don't expect to live to middle age, who take risks because living to be twenty-five is not a reality in their lives. When this uncertainty about living to adulthood gets combined, as it often does, with a sense of despair, our boys are capable of taking risks which can only be considered suicidal. You can find them in gangs from one end of the country to the other. Boys who through their own experience know the odds of dying—or being shot, or being imprisoned—outweigh those that they will graduate from high school. Many of these boys see no way out, they don't even hope for a better life, and instead of acting cautiously, they act even more recklessly. Their bodies fill our prisons and our morgues across America.

The need for risk is understood by the commercial marketeers who exploit it. Have you seen the soft drink commercial where teenage boys are shown competing with one another on mountain bikes to see who can perform the most reckless, death-defying stunt? It's not enough for one of them to ride at break-neck speed down a mountain trail that even a goat would find hard to negotiate; that stunt just gets a "done that" from the other boys. It's only when one boy literally rides his bike off a cliff, his life saved by a parachute attached to his back, that the others acknowledge that a sufficient level of risk has been reached. The message is clear: the fun, the real fun, begins only when you've crossed the boundary of safety. Commercials emphasizing these new extreme forms of sport support the notion that whether riding a bike, skiing, or riding a skateboard, if you're not jumping, flipping, or hurtling through the air, you're not doing "what boys do."

I am convinced that boys are going to take risks whether we want them to or not. Just visit any amusement park and see which ride has the longest lines; it will be the roller coaster. It seems many of us want to take perceived risks, to do things which while we are doing them seem dangerous but which we know are really safe. For boys, this fascination with risk doesn't stop when they leave the amusement park. They often create their own adventures without being able to predict the safe ending guaranteed by the roller coaster. When my brothers and I were young we jumped from the limb of an old tree in the backyard holding onto an umbrella, convinced that the physics of this feat, performed by cartoon characters who jumped off cliffs with umbrellas and landed safely all the time, would work for us too. It took several crash landings before we understood that to climb higher in the tree for a longer jump might end in disaster. Some years later my youngest brother, Reuben, broke his arm jumping from the second floor of an abandoned building onto an old mattress we had found. This was an extension of the umbrella experiment. It worked well for us until a slight miscalculation sent him to the hospital.

If boys are going to take risks, the challenge is to structure those risks so that boys fulfill their need to flirt with danger, yet, as with the roller coaster, we can predict that they will not injure themselves or somebody else. This means that we must ensure that boys have the opportunity to get involved with activities that contain controlled risks. The hard thing is to offer a range of activities so that they have real choices. Some boys will find that football offers enough of a challenge, for some it may be the martial arts, for some rock climbing, for some playing a solo on the trumpet in front of an audience. And because peer groups play such an important role in risk-taking behavior, it is important that these activities be set up to allow boys to spend time just making friends with others who are involved in the same kind of positive endeavor.

We must teach boys how to properly evaluate when a risk is fun and harmless, and when it is dangerous. Too often boys do things without thinking. They never meant to get involved with something dangerous or illegal, they just went along with the crowd. Boys are not taught how to say no to their friends. So many boys would be alive today—or not locked up in jail, or not addicted to drugs—if they had just learned how to evaluate what they were being asked to participate in. But we can't expect boys to "just say no" every time. Boys who don't have structured activities in their free time, *and* caring adults who set and enforce limits, often will not, and cannot, say no. We have to structure an environment that allows them to say yes to so many things that are exciting and challenging that they end up with too many choices that are positive to dwell on the ones that are negative. There are too many boys in America who, after school or during the summer, find all they have is the equivalent of what we had as children—an old beat-up mattress, a second-story window, and a need for adventure. In a world where dangers proliferate, the results are predictable.

Self-Worth

EVERY YEAR I try to find out what is the latest fashion trend for boys. It's not that I find the changing styles particularly interesting, it's that I know that in New York City, and in cities all across this country, boys will be robbed, and in the process threatened, beaten, or even killed, because they were wearing the latest "gear." One year it was shearling coats (costing over two hundred dollars), one year Starter brand jackets (jackets that carry professional team names on the back), and every year it's the latest sneaker. Part of our job at Rheedlen is to make sure that we constantly warn children about the dangers inherent in buying and wearing the expensive gear that others might try to take by force.

The pressure on children, especially poor boys, to wear the latest styles has grown overwhelmingly over the years. These boys represent an important market to clothing manufacturers, and poor inner-city youth help set the trends in clothing wear across this country and around the world. Millions of dollars are spent on advertising to entice these boys to buy Nike, or Reebok, or a host of other brand names, and the connection between what you wear and what you are is created for them by some of the most sophisticated marketing minds in America.

The pressure on boys to conform, to fit in, grows as they get older. This is not new—what's new is the extent to which advertisers take advantage of it. There was pressure to dress a certain way even when I was a young boy, before the advent of the nonstop mega-marketing to boys that exists today. In fact, I remember when this industry trend was just beginning. I was in grade school, and where before I cared nothing about what I wore, suddenly things began to change in regards to clothes. It was not just me but the other boys and girls my age who began to become interested in certain types and styles of clothing.

At this time, in the early sixties, the biggest fashion issue for boys was sneakers. My mother would buy our tennis shoes from John's Bargain store on Third Avenue in the Bronx, where for $1.99 you could get one of several types. I was in the fifth grade and I needed sneakers. I wanted P. F. Flyers because I was sure they would make me the fastest boy on the block. My mother explained that they were too expensive, and so it was the John's Bargain store brand for all four of us. I was a little disappointed about not getting P. F. Flyers, but new sneakers were still pretty exciting. That day I raced outside in my brand-new pair of white sneakers to test how fast I could run and how high I could jump. I was pleased when a group of older boys with some of my friends called me over. I ran over with what I thought was just the right amount of drama, jumped high in the air, and landed with a squeak of rubber on cement as I came to a screeching stop. Just to make sure no one missed my new sneakers, I stood on one leg and stretched a foot as far forward as possible.

Robert said with a deceiving sweetness, "Gee, Geoff, I see you got yourself a brand-new pair of skips." Everyone began to laugh.

I didn't get it. What were "skips"? Robert saw his opening and pressed his assault. "Geoff, I bet you can *skip* faster than everybody here." More laughter. Suddenly it dawned on me that they were talking about my brand-new sneakers. I knew how to handle this.

"Well, I bet you can't beat me running in my sneakers. They're made for running, you know. C'mon, let's race."

"Okay. I'll run, you skip." More laughter. "Where did you get those cheap things? John's Bargain?" More laughter.

"Your sneakers are cheaper than mine. If I got mine at John Bargain's you got yours at the cheap welfare store." No laughter.

Robert replied with a braggart's confidence. "No, these are Converse. I got them at the Army and Navy store. They cost me eleven dollars. These ain't no skips." All the other boys began to admire his new sneakers. And he broke out in song. "If your sneakers slip and slide, get the ones with the star on the side. Con-verse!"

And there it was, as big as life. A star on the ankle of his new Converse All-Stars. The fact that none of the other boys had shoes like these didn't seem to faze anyone. They all began to say how they were "going to get me a pair right away." Their mothers or fathers would certainly buy each of them a pair of Converse sneakers, but there I was with brand-new skips on and no hope for any other pair for a long time. My first day in my new sneakers was ruined. From seemingly nowhere Converse was the sneaker to have. It seemed that every day a new boy on our block or the surrounding blocks got a new pair of Converses. And skips ownership became synonymous with the wearer being not only poor but totally out of style. Some days I didn't even go outside, the teasing would be so fierce. Luckily, you couldn't wear sneakers to school (certainly not the case today), so at least the teasing was confined to after school. Things got better when my skips got older. Then I could say, as the other boys had, "My mother said she was gonna get me a pair of Cons when this pair wears out." I thought this was true, even though I hadn't yet discussed my next pair of sneakers with my mother. How could she not buy me Cons? I was sure she loved me as much as Robert's mother loved him, or Billy's mother loved him. Their families didn't have any money, either. In fact, they were on welfare and my mother had a job.

By the age of ten I was very aware of our precarious financial situation. My mother was honest with us about how much money she made as a secretary. Trying to raise four boys on twenty-five dollars a week was no easy task. Putting food on the table and clothes on our backs, and paying the rent, electric bill, gas bill, and phone bill left her with a disposable income that was usually four or five dollars a week. It was from this small pot that we all received whatever treats or special favors we could convince her to buy us. With four of us competing for such a small amount of money, she was constantly setting priorities and explaining why we couldn't afford this or that.

My mother taught us how to stretch a dollar way beyond what others thought was possible. I hated to shop for my clothes with her because we would visit every department store and clothing store on Third Avenue looking for the best value. And because my mother knew how to sew she could tell if something was put together cheaply. So if you wanted a particular shirt you not only had to find the best price, it had to pass her intense scrutiny. She was forever calling me over and saying, "Look at that seam. Just look at it. That wouldn't last you two weeks before you would bust it. I'm not going to waste my hard-earned money on trash like this. C'mon, we'll look someplace else. Alexander's is only three blocks away." And the fact that I dragged my feet and hung my head at the thought of walking three more blocks and visiting what I knew would be store after store just for one stupid shirt made no impression on my mother at all. But it didn't take me long once I was working as a teenager and had bought a pair of shoes at the first store I came to, only to see the same shoe for two dollars less a couple of blocks away, to learn the value of her shopping strategy. Even to this day no one wants to shop with me because I go from store to store looking for the best value possible.

Still, at ten years old I thought my mother was the cheapest person in the world, and I knew the opposition I would be facing in trying to get her to give me eleven dollars to buy Converse sneakers. My mother and I were very close, and not only did I know how dire our financial situation was, I also knew my mother's most likely responses to every request for money for nonessential items. So I needed to devise a strategy to penetrate her monetary defense system, a system so formidable that I knew it would take the equivalent of a stealth bomber to separate her from that eleven dollars. My request would take serious planning and perfect timing.

At last my sneakers had their first hole in the sole and I had my setup. "Ma, I need some new sneakers."

"I just bought you those sneakers. They can't be ruined already."

"No, that was Reuben. I had these things forever. Remember when you got them at John's Bargain? I done had these things for almost a year."

"What's wrong with them? They look all right to me."

"Look. They got a hole in the bottom. They ain't no good no more."

"Don't say 'ain't.' Oh, I see. They do have a hole. Lord, how you all go through sneakers. Well you're going to have to wait, I just bought a pair of sneakers for your brother and I don't have money right now. Maybe next week."

"But Ma, they got a hole in them. My feet get wet and I might step on a piece a glass or something."

"You're just going to have to put a piece of cardboard in them to get through the next week."

I hung my head slightly, said, "All right," found the scissors, and began to look for a nice thick piece of cardboard. We all had done the cardboard thing, and through trial and error knew what type of cardboard would last the longest. Having a hole in your sneaker or shoe was at least better than having the sole come loose—then the kids would tease you about the noise it made as it slapped against the pavement or floor. Getting new soles on shoes costs almost as much as a new pair, so the only thing to do was to cut off the part of the sole that was flapping, which meant that pretty soon you'd get a hole in the now sole-less thin layer of leather between your foot and the pavement. That you could handle with cardboard again, and since other kids couldn't tell if you had cardboard in your shoe, the teasing would stop.

So far the plan was going just fine. I wore the sneakers with the cardboard in them for a week and asked for new sneakers again. My mother still didn't have the money. She asked if I could make it another week. I said yes. That next week I hardly went outside. Every time my mother asked me what was wrong I just shrugged my shoulders and said, "Nothing." I watched my mother begin to get worried about me. She was beginning, I could tell, to feel bad. She told me that she would definitely get me a new pair of sneakers with her next paycheck. I sighed and walked to the window, looked out, and politely refused her suggestion that I go out and play. She was set up, it was time to go in for the kill.

My mother got paid on Fridays and Fridays were our favorite day of the week. We all waited downstairs for my mother to get home from work and she would always buy us a soda. If she was in a really good mood she'd give us each an extra quarter. We lived for Fridays. On this particular Friday, though, I was not downstairs with my three brothers. When my mother came into the apartment with the groceries as always on Friday, I was waiting there. She knew something was wrong with me right away.

"Why didn't you meet me downstairs? Come here, I have fifty cents for you."

"Thanks, but I don't want anything."

This was unheard of, any of us refusing money. "Geoff, what's wrong? You been acting funny all week."

"Ma, the other kids have been teasing me. Every time I go outside they laugh at me. I feel ashamed."

"Honey, what are you ashamed about? Don't tell me, let me guess. Your sneakers, right? Well, don't worry, I put aside two dollars for you to get some new sneakers."

"It's not that. Everybody's teasing me about wearing sneakers from John's Bargain. I need to get a different kind of sneaker. Ma, can I get a pair of Converse sneakers? All the kids are wearing them. They are really good sneakers and last for more than a year. I would do anything to get a pair. I'll wash the dishes, take out the garbage, clean up the apartment—anything. Can I get a pair, Ma? Can I?"

There it was. I'd taken my time to set things up as best as possible, and now I'd made my pitch. My mother said uncertainly, "Well, Geoff, I don't know. I only have a couple of dollars."

Now it was time to launch my stealth missiles directly to her heart. "Ma, I just can't go outside and play with those cheap sneakers anymore. The kids won't play with me. They talk about me. They call you cheap, Ma. I almost had to fight Charles for talking about you. Please, Ma. Please."

My mother looked trapped. She wanted the best for all of us and she knew how tough kids could be on one another. I could see her resolve crumbling. "Well I don't . . . I mean, how could they . . . well, how much do they cost?"

This was the moment I had been planning for two weeks.

Careful now. So close. Don't blow it. "They cost eleven dollars, but I . . ."

"Eleven dollars! Eleven dollars! Boy, are you crazy? I ain't giving you no eleven dollars to put on your feet."

"Ma, you said 'ain't.'" She didn't smile. "Come on, Ma. I have to have a pair of Converse."

"I don't care if I said 'ain't,' or 'not,' or 'won't,' 'can't,' 'will never,' or anything else. You won't get no eleven dollars from me. Do you know how much I make a week? If I gave you eleven dollars we would all starve."

This wasn't going too well. Time to change plans. "Ma, everybody else's mother buys them Cons. Don't you love me? If you really loved me you would get me some Converse."

"Geoff. Now listen to me. I love you, son. But eleven-dollar sneakers have nothing to do with love. And I don't care what the other mothers are doing for their children. You are my child. I am much more interested in what goes into your head than what goes on your feet. Eleven-dollar sneakers will not get you out of high school or into college. I can't afford eleven-dollar sneakers. And you know what? Even if I could I wouldn't buy them. It's a waste of good money. No sneaker could be worth eleven dollars. Now here's three dollars to buy some sneakers. You can buy whatever kind you like."

So far all my strategy had produced was one measly extra dollar. It was time for a new tactic. "Ma, I can't go outside again. I just can't take it. You're so mean to me." With that I ran crying into the room I shared with my brother and threw myself on the bed. I could hear my mother making dinner as I cried for what seemed to me to be forever. My mother, if she noticed my crying, acted as if she didn't. I worked on her for three more days. After a while I had to admit to myself that my plan was not going to work. My mother meant it. Finally she said if I wasn't going to spend the three dollars she would take it back. Reluctantly I went downtown to buy a pair of sneakers. At least with three dollars I didn't have to go to John's Bargain. I bought a pair of skips that looked more like Cons, but they didn't fool any of the kids on the block for a second. Once again I was the butt of many jokes. By now the block was divided into those kids who had Converse sneakers and those who, like myself, were unable to get their parents to part with eleven dollars. We developed strategies to counter the teasing. The first thing you did with a new pair of skips was to dirty them up so they weren't so noticeable. Then we all swore to the other boys this would be our last pair of skips, that our mothers had promised us Cons when these wore out. We were met with a great deal of skepticism, but we stuck to that story.

I was in the sixth grade when I got my first pair of Converse sneakers. I earned the money myself by walking a dog for one of my mother's friends and by selling newspapers. I didn't go to the Army and Navy store and pay eleven dollars for my Cons. I walked an extra ten blocks to a store on Southern Boulevard where you could get Converse "seconds" for nine dollars. When I put those sneakers on I was the proudest boy on Union Avenue.

The sneaker craze of today was in its infancy back in 1961, and the fad for Converse and later for Pro Ked sneakers was then driven almost completely by word of mouth in inner cities across America. There were no Michael Jordans or Shaquille O'Neals extolling the virtues of their sneakers the way it is today. Today the pressure on boys to buy the latest in fashion trends is much more powerful than when I was a teenager. And the pressure on the child soon becomes pressure on the parent. Parents who have the money— and parents who don't—find that they are constantly besieged by their sons to buy articles of clothing that have more expense than value, and that they are constantly overpaying for clothing, sometimes to the extreme.

Parents should know that it is more than peer pressure that is creating this need to wear brand names. The advertisers of the world have become expert in manipulating the minds of our children, especially our boys. They teach them early to develop an insatiable hunger for name-brand stuff, a hunger that has no connection to value, or reliability, or to anything else. In fact, the opposite is the case; clothing and sneaker companies change styles so quickly that kids rarely get to wear anything out anymore, so they learn nothing about value. Our children are becoming robotic consumers, buying without thinking, carelessly discarding items that are perfectly fine—people who associate their self-worth with what they are wearing, or driving, or even eating.

The concern I have is not just about what we buy boys to wear, it is about all kinds of items we buy them. Some parents have bought every toy, or video, or CD imaginable. The problem is that so much of the buying and giving happens without our boys feeling that they have earned it. Instead, they feel entitled to hundred-dollar sneakers or two-hundred-dollar video games. And this sense of entitlement runs counter to the way many of us were raised. Many of us had to work hard, sacrifice, and save for long periods of time for what we wanted. Have we forgotten how good we felt and how much we valued something that it took us a long time to earn? Our drive to succeed and to work hard for what we wanted was often instilled early, by our parents.

It's not the end of the world for boys to learn how to cope with being teased by their peers. If they don't learn early on how to resist the pressures their peers put on them, later it won't be hundred-dollar sneakers, but beer or drugs or sex. And what happens when you've bought all the toys, all the clothes, all the video games, and that boy turns twelve or thirteen? Where does he get that constant stimulation from then? Where is the "feel good all the time" feeling going to come from?

Boys are a prime target for ruthless marketing that constantly attempts to persuade them that their self-worth, their happiness, and even their manhood is tied to what they buy. Many have not had the training and support that is needed to create a self-image that can withstand the constant assault of peers and advertisers. Boys need a sense of self that is developed through personal accomplishments and hard work. A sense of self that includes the desire to grow into men who are kind, disciplined, and caring. Someone must spend the time making sure that they know we care more about the quality of their hearts and their spirits than we do about their clothes and their haircuts. And they must find support for their sense of self-worth on a regular basis. It must be reinforced over and over again, because it will constantly be under attack from outside forces. So many boys' self-worth is defined by people trying to sell them something, and they don't know where to turn, or who to turn to, to discover their true self-worth. So many adults have forgotten that this is *our* job.

Fatherhood

I HAVE SIX SONS. Jerry is my genetic son, Bruce is my stepson, and I have four young men I call my sons whom I've helped raise since they were young boys. I have one daughter, Melina, and two adopted daughters who are young women in college now. My sons and daughters would tell you that I am a tough father, that I push them to do better and am never satisfied with a mediocre effort. Jerry has just completed law school at Berkeley; another one of my sons, a high school dropout when I met him, has completed college and wants to go to law school. My other sons are either in college or working. Jerry recently got married and he and his wife, Johanny, have just had a baby boy, Justin. On Father's Day he wrote me a letter, part of which said, "The father you've been over the years has provided me with guidance, kindness, and a relationship that only a father and son could have. And as I have become a father this year I hope and pray that my son will one day look upon me with the same feelings and appreciation I have for you and experience the same pride."

As I read Jerry's letter I felt a great sense of pride in my son.

Maybe it's because I grew up without a father, maybe it's because I just believe this deeply, but I have always told my sons that if they have a child they must never be anything but an active father to that child. To hear my son wanting his own son to love him, appreciate him, and have pride in him, made me feel that I had accomplished part of my goal in raising my sons, instilling in them a fierce sense of paternity. But I was stopped by the words "a relationship that only a father and son could have." A relationship I never had, one millions of boys won't have.

I had seldom thought about my father since his not-so-sudden death from cirrhosis of the liver. He had been steadily drinking himself to death for many years, so it was not a surprise to me when I heard that he had died. As young boys my brothers and I were not close to our father. Like most children, we desperately wanted an intact family. But we found out early on that our father was hopelessly addicted to alcohol and that everything else in his life was secondary to his bottle. When we asked our mother why he had left us, she stated flatly, "I put him out." She explained that she'd been tired of his coming home on payday without enough money to pay the rent, leaving her to worry about what to tell the landlord. Too often we'd had our lights turned off, and we'd lost our apartment several times. Enough was enough. She explained to us early on what an alcoholic was. She might have been angry with my father for leaving her to raise four boys by herself, but if she was she never let on to us about it. She explained that even though she had to put him out, our father was a very intelligent man who had a good heart.

My brothers and I all had very different relationships with our absent father. Dan was the one who every couple of years would look up our father and visit him. John seemed to give up on him, never going to see him again once he left. Reuben, the youngest, would tag along on some of the visits that were made over the years, but never seemed to care much one way or the other. I was probably the most ambivalent. The first time Dan decided to go visit, our father was living in Harlem. I was about ten years old. Dan asked our mother if we could visit him and she said it was all right. We called him and told him we were coming. Dan and I took the train to Harlem and found my father's building. He was the superintendent and lived in the basement apartment with his second wife and their child, our stepbrother, Johnny-Mac. I didn't know what to expect. The only memories I had of my father were vague, dreamlike images of him in our old apartment. I had a fantasy that we would walk into his apartment and find a relatively well-off man who would open his arms and say, "Here are my boys. Come give Daddy a hug," and we would sheepishly walk into his wide embrace.

The fantasy didn't last long. The basement apartment was small and sparsely furnished. My father was drinking something out of a cup. He looked somewhat pained to see us. He knew Daniel right away. He looked at me and said, "Now, are you Johnny or Geoffrey?"

"I'm Geoffrey," I said. I was disappointed that my own father didn't even know who I was.

The talk stayed polite and revolved around what grades we were in, what sports we played, that kind of thing. After a few minutes we ran out of conversation. He asked us if we wanted to play cards. Dan said yes. I just watched. They played gin rummy. My father relaxed into the card game, and he bantered about this and that and was full of wisecracks. As the hours went by I found, surprisingly, that I liked him. He obviously wasn't remotely successful, but he was fun to be around and he was intelligent. The problem was that I didn't know whether he liked me. He seemed to feel close to Dan, but besides throwing a few jokes my way, he seemed totally neutral toward me. When we left he asked Dan when he would visit again, but he simply said goodbye to me.

I left feeling more confused than when I'd come. This man was my father, but he didn't seem to feel any particular way about me. The real issue was that he didn't seem to love me. Could you be somebody's father and not love him? I knew he didn't know me and I thought if he really took the time to know me, he probably would love me. But he didn't seem to want to get to know me. Before our visit, I imagined I would be able to feel that special parental bond that exists between a child and a parent. It might not be obvious to others, but I knew I would be able to sense it from a look he would give me, or the way he would rub my head, or something. But when I met him there was nothing. No hugs, no physical contact of any kind, no words of endearment, no special glances. He didn't have any money to give us when we left, not even a quarter. I rode back to the Bronx wondering how a man could have four children and never come to see them or even call to see how they were doing. He just seemed not to care.

You can imagine my surprise when one day about three months later my brother Dan told me he had spoken to my father and that he'd said he had a bicycle for me. Dan had a bike and often would ride me all over the Bronx, me riding sidesaddle on the crossbar. We would get up at five in the morning on a Saturday, before people came outside, before the cars took over the streets, and ride for hours. We thought of ourselves as explorers, finding neighborhoods we had never seen before, going down to the Third Avenue business district to watch the workers unload their wares. But sooner or later, no matter how much fun we were having, Daniel would get tired from pedaling the bicycle with my extra weight on it and I would get sore from sitting on the narrow crossbar. So our adventures always ended before we were ready to call it a day. I would always think, "If only I had a bicycle for me. Then we could be real explorers." And now my prayers were answered. My father had a bike for me.

I was overjoyed about the bicycle. But I was just as happy to know that my father, a man who the last time I visited hadn't known my name, was thinking about me. My doubts about whether he loved me were not fully assuaged, but I now knew he at least liked me, thought about me, wanted to do something for me. My brothers John and Reuben asked if he had something for them also. They had assumed that Dan's and my going to see him was a big waste of time.

Dan answered, "He didn't say anything about you all. He said he had a bike for Geoffrey. He got it from somebody in his building."

"Yeah," I chimed in. "He ain't got nothing for you two. You didn't come to see him. I told you to come. I told you he was all right."

It was hard for me to keep the gloating from my voice. Secretly I was happy that my father didn't have any gifts for his other sons. "Maybe," I thought, "he'll come to like me the best. Maybe even more than Dan." I couldn't help but daydream about walks and talks my father and I would have. Just a boy and his father, talking about things fathers and sons talk about. And the more selfish side of me thought, "How many really good things could people give away in my father's building? Certainly not enough for my brothers *and* me." In my daydreams, after we walked and talked, my father would take me back to his building and say, "Geoffrey, I have a little something for you." Then he would reach on top of the refrigerator and pull down a slightly used baseball glove.

"You know, it's not new," he would say. "But it's hardly been used. Come on outside and let me throw you a few fast ones."

"But I can't catch too good," I would confide to my father. "The kids are always giving me a hard time because I sometimes drop the ball."

"Do you have on a glove when you drop the ball?" he would inquire.

"Sometimes. Sometimes the other kids let me borrow one of their gloves."

"Well, that's the problem. A boy has to have his own glove. That way you get used to it. It becomes part of your body. Don't worry, I'll teach you how to catch. Wait until you go back on the block and the other kids see you in action. Do you know how to handle a hot line drive?"

I would shake my head and my father would simply say, "C'mon outside, boy, you've got a lot to learn." These daydreams always left me with a warm feeling. I felt that suddenly there was another powerful person in my life.

As the weekend approached when Dan and I would return to pick up my bicycle, I thought more about my father than I had in a long time. In the early sixties the crisis of black men walking away from their families was already an evident reality in poor neighborhoods like the one I lived in. But it hadn't grown to the proportions you see today in these same neighborhoods. There were still fathers on the block. And while some of my friends had fathers, we couldn't quite figure out if in the end their families were that much better off than the families of those of us who didn't. The fathers who lived on my block were not the same type of fathers we saw on television shows like *Leave It to Beaver*, or *Father Knows Best*, or *My Three Sons*. These were men who helped their sons, talked with them, did things with them. The fathers on our block were spoken of in hushed tones. You never saw them outside teaching their children to roller-skate or play football. When my friends talked about their fathers it was usually in the context of discipline. Fathers, we were told, hit harder than mothers. They were hard characters who demanded quiet when they came home from work, and quick and complete obedience to their every demand, and who expected mother and child to act respectful and even fearful.

But even with the drawbacks that we heard of, every boy wanted to have a father. Many times I heard tales from my friends that their mother had said no to buying a football, but their father had said yes. When the mother and father got into a fight over money and the fact that the family could not afford a football, the father would be the one to say, "Don't you worry. I'll buy my son a football myself." And just like that, we would be playing in the churchyard with a brand-new football. How I longed to have a father say those magic words for me—"I'm going to buy my son a football." I would come blazing back to Union Avenue, football tucked under my arm, and when everyone asked where I got a brand-new leather ball (not the cheap plastic kind some kids tried to pretend were real footballs), I would quietly say, "My father bought it for me."

There was another distinct advantage the kids with fathers had over those of us who didn't have them. The older boys dared not bother a boy with a father. Fathers would come downstairs in a rage if some older boy beat up their son. I had seen the way my father acted on the street and I could tell he didn't take no stuff off nobody. Wouldn't all the other boys be surprised when my father came back to the Bronx with me and came on the block? Everyone would come up and ask me who he was. I couldn't wait to tell them he was my father. Then I would wait until Robert came outside. Robert was the primary tormentor of little boys on the block. He was always picking on us. I couldn't *wait* for the day Robert met my father. I couldn't wait to see what Robert's face would look like when my father told him, "You better not bother my son again or else I'm going to come on this block and beat you up." Robert would die. And I knew Robert didn't have a father, so there would be nobody for him to get to go after my dad. When my father showed up on the block I would be treated differently from that point on.

The Saturday finally arrived when it was time for me to go to my father's and get my bicycle. Daniel offered to ride me on the crossbar of his bicycle so that we could ride back from Harlem to the Bronx together. We left early to try to beat most of the traffic because we had to ride over the Third Avenue Bridge to get into Harlem from the Bronx. I had never been on a bicycle in highway traffic, and the cars and trucks were doing forty and fifty miles an hour across the bridge. Dan was pedaling as hard as he could to try and stay with the flow of traffic. Riding on the crossbar with my hands on the handlebar, I could look both in front and behind us. I have never been more terrified in my life. I could hear Dan's heavy breathing in my ear as he pumped the pedals as fast as he could. Cars were moving past us at a steady pace. Suddenly, behind us I saw a huge tractor-trailer. The driver was waving at us to get out of the way. He was signaling me to have Dan pull the bicycle over to the right because he wanted to make a right-hand turn.

"Dan! Dan, pull over! That man in the truck behind us wants you to pull over!"

"I can't pull over. We're not getting off on the right. We have to go straight," Dan said.

Just then the man in the truck reached above his head and pulled on the cord that sounded the horn. I had never heard a tractor-trailer horn before. The deep resonating sound signaled imminent doom to me.

"Dan, pull over! He's gonna crash us!" I screamed, looking behind Dan's head at the now malevolent face of the trucker who was pulling his horn over and over again, making a deafening noise.

Dan stood up and started pumping harder and harder. He started laughing. I couldn't believe it. We were about to be killed by a huge monster truck and Daniel was laughing.

"He's not going to crash us," Dan said between his fits of laughter. "Turn around. Look straight ahead. We're going to make it. We're almost there. Turn around I said!" he shouted at me, even as the wind seemed to snatch his words away before they hit my ear. I turned and looked straight ahead. Dan was right. I could now see the exit we were trying to get to. I heard the screeching of brakes as the trucker slowed his rig so he wouldn't run over the two crazy boys on one bicycle who sped straight ahead as he exited to the right.

When we were off the bridge and on the relatively quiet streets of Spanish Harlem, I asked Dan, "What were you doing back there? You could have gotten us both killed."

He laughed again. "No, you're wrong. I've done this before. The first time I was scared like you. A big truck came up behind me and I panicked and went off to the right. Once you do that it takes forever to get back into Harlem. So I learned. If they think they can scare you they will. But if you act like you aren't scared, then they slow up or go around you. Now I want you to remember. We have to go back home the same way. No matter what you do, don't take that exit off. I don't care how many times they blow their horn or how close they get to you, don't get off to the right. Understand?" I nodded my head yes. I was already dreading the trip home.

The rest of the ride to my father's building was uneventful. Once we arrived I took a closer look at the building in which my father worked and lived. I was noticing it for the first time. On my first visit I'd been too excited to have paid any attention to it. The building was not much different from the one we lived in. It was like ours, a six-story walk-up with dingy halls and bare lightbulbs hanging from ceiling fixtures that had seen better days. The hallways were narrower. And our building was almost exclusively African-American, but this one was mostly Latino. The tenants in my father's building looked no better off than the ones who lived in ours. It was, I knew, a rare occasion when someone threw away a perfectly good item as expensive as a bicycle in our building; when something like a bicycle was completely unrepairable, it was taken apart and used to replace damaged or broken parts on other bikes. As I really saw the building, I began to have doubts that the bicycle that my father had scavenged was the sleek, shiny, three-speed model I had imagined up until that point.

Daniel and I went down the stairs to my father's basement apartment. He was out when we got there, but his wife, Bernice, told us he was working and would be back any minute. The minutes crawled by like hours. Finally he arrived. When he saw us he seemed surprised, as if he wasn't expecting us to be there. We sat around the small kitchen table, drank Kool Aid out of old jelly jars, and made the same type of small talk we had on the first visit. My father asked if we wanted to play cards. Not another game of five-hundred gin rummy, I groaned inwardly, that could take forever. And it did. They played. I watched. The game dragged on. Finally it was over. Not once up to this point did my father mention my bicycle. Daniel, sensing my growing impatience, said, "Well, it's time for us to go now," and stood up from the table. My father stood up also.

"Well, it's good to see you. Come by to see me again."

That was it. The visit was over. I looked at Daniel, my eyes imploring him to ask what suddenly I couldn't. I had lost the power of speech. I opened my mouth but nothing came out. "Where's the bike?" I wanted to shout. "I came here to get my bike. Have you forgotten?" Instead my mouth opened and then closed. "Dan, save me. Ask him about the bike," my eyes begged my older brother.

"Er . . . you know, you said you had something for Geoffrey," Dan said, picking up on my desperation.

"What? Something for Geoffrey?" My father looked uncertain.

"A bike. You said you had a bike for me," I was finally able to say, speaking much too loudly.

"Oh yeah. The bike. The bike I got out of the trash. Yeah, I still got it. Unless someone done gone and taken it from the trash room. C'mon, it's probably still there." He walked toward the door and we followed.

How could he have left my bike in the trash room, I wondered. Why didn't he bring it into his apartment and keep it safe for me? "Please be there," I prayed.

We walked into a dark, dank basement area that contained the boiler, a mountain of coal, and trash cans lined up against one wall. The room smelled of rotting garbage and urine. I peered all around, looking for signs of a bicycle. I didn't see one. My father kept walking, past the boiler, past the coal, to another, smaller room. Inside there were some broken pieces of furniture, old tires, and, to my heart's delight, a bicycle. My father picked up the bike and said, "Let's go outside." He led the procession back through the trash room, up the stairs, and back onto the street. As we walked I couldn't believe it. I had my own bicycle. Now I would be able to ride with my brother and to explore the world. We would be real explorers. We would go everywhere.

Once up the stairs I ran over to my father and the bicycle. He was wiping dust and dirt off the frame with a rag he had picked up on his way outside. I looked at the bike and my heart sank. My father saw the change in my demeanor and tried to cheer me up.

"Look, it ain't so bad. So it's got a flat tire—that can be changed. And the handlebars are a little crooked, but look, I can straighten that out right now. The gears work . . . well . . . I think they work. Let's just push this . . . it's coming . . . it's coming . . . er, well, a little oil, that's what it needs. And don't worry about the missing pedal. That piece of metal they put there will get you home. A little work and it'll be like brand-new," he said with a not quite convincing smile.

I thought to myself, "A little work and it'll be a piece of shit." I looked to Dan for some help or some understanding of what had happened to my dream. He seemed to be in the same state of shock I was.

"Well, listen, I have some things to get back to. Will you all be all right getting the bikes back home?" my father asked even as he began to walk away.

"Yeah, we'll be just great. Don't worry about us," I said with all the sarcasm I could muster. If my father heard the hurt or disappointment in my voice he certainly showed no signs of it as he disappeared back down the basement steps. Once he had descended back into his life and out of ours, I crumpled down on the curb, my elbows on my knees and palms cradling my face. I was glad my father had left before I started to cry. Crying in front of him would have added to the shame I was feeling for believing so desperately in the fantasy of my father's love. How were we supposed to get home with that junk he said was a bike? He wasn't even going to try to help me fix it. He just left. Left, like all was great. Left, like he was in the running for the father of the year award. Left, like a twelve-year-old and a ten-year-old could manage a broken bike and a long trip home with no problem.

Daniel knew I was despondent. I looked at him as he studied what was now my bike. He had what I thought of as his scientific look on his face. This was the same look I'd seen when he was dissecting a goldfish that had died and been found floating belly up in the fish tank. The same look he'd had when he had taken apart our broken Christmas present that we loved, Robot Commando.

"C'mon, Geoff, it ain't so bad," he said to me as he looked at the bicycle. Suddenly the absurdity of what he'd said hit him. "Yes it is," he said. "This is a piece of shit." And he started laughing.

I got so angry with him when he started laughing. This wasn't funny. We had come all the way over here to get a broken-down bike. My father had just left us without even trying to help. He didn't love me, he didn't even care. And there was Daniel, laughing. Then I remembered him laughing at the tractor-trailer truck. There was my older brother, the closest thing I had to a father. He didn't have any money, he couldn't beat up the older boys who threatened and terrorized us, but he could show me how to face adversity. You could laugh in its face and pedal harder. Suddenly I looked around me. We were in a strange neighborhood, two bikes standing on the sidewalk, me crying on the curb, and Daniel laughing like a madman. I started to chuckle. Daniel looked at me, then pointed to the bike.

"It's a piece of shit," he said. And as he looked at the smile creeping across my face he doubled over laughing, holding his stomach. I couldn't help it, I began to laugh too. We both laughed uncontrollably for quite a while. Finally I looked at Daniel and asked, "Can you fix it?"

"I think so. I have a patch kit in my saddlebag. If we can find a gas station with an air pump, I think I can fix the flat. The handlebars are a little loose, but I think we can get the bike home like that. The gear shift is stuck in three, which means it's going to be hard to pedal at first, and forget going up any steep hills, we'll have to walk. The tires are real bad, but I think we can get home."

The ride home was traumatic for me. We pushed the bikes to a local gas station and Daniel repaired the tire. He rode my bike because he was the more skilled rider and didn't want me to get hurt. I rode his. As we were coming across the bridge that would bring us back into the Bronx from Manhattan, another tractor-trailer pulled up behind us and the driver started blowing his horn. Daniel, who was in the lead, yelled back at me to keep going, not to turn off to the right. I tried to be strong and laugh at the trucker the way Dan had, but I got scared. Dan stood up and started pedaling harder, the way he had earlier that day.

He yelled at me, "Don't look back! C'mon."

But I did look back. There was the trucker glaring at me. I could see him cursing. The truck lurched forward and he signaled me to get over to the right. I turned and looked straight ahead. Dan had pulled away. He was more than thirty yards ahead of me. He had already passed the right-hand exit. I was all alone, just me and the crazy truck driver. I looked back and almost fell off my bike. The truck was only a few feet from my back tire. The driver, sitting way above me, was cursing me even as he accelerated the truck toward me. I didn't want to die. I turned off to the right. The truck came barreling past, horn blaring, wheels throwing dust and dirt in my face. I pulled off the exit and realized I had no idea where I was. Daniel was out of sight, and I remembered he had told me it was very difficult to get back home from this exit. I sat down and began to cry for the second time that day. I looked up the ramp toward the bridge where cars and trucks were whizzing past. There was no way I was going to be able to get up enough speed to enter that traffic again. I would have to try to make it home alone the best way I could and hope I didn't run into a group of boys who would take Dan's bike or beat me up.

I took one last look up the exit ramp and couldn't help but grin when I saw Daniel. He had ridden his bike against the traffic to come and find me. I was never so happy to see someone in my life.

"Dan!" I yelled. "Dan, you came back for me!"

"Of course I came back for you. You didn't think I was going to just leave you, did you?" The question was rhetorical. "That truck scared you, huh? Don't worry, you did okay. He was a mean one, that guy. I saw him laughing at you when he made you turn off. C'mon, let's go." He started back up the ramp the way he had come.

"Go? Go where? You don't expect me to go back up there, do you?"

"Of course. How else are we going to get home?"

"I can't do it, Dan. I'm scared. I can't go back. Can't we get home another way?"

"The other way takes too long. Plus I don't really know how I got home that time. I just rode around until I found a street that looked familiar. It might take us hours. I know you're scared, but trust me, they're not going to run you down. We just have a little way to go. We'll wait until we see a break in the traffic. We can do it. Let's go."

With that we walked our bikes back up the ramp with car horns blaring, warning us we were going the wrong way into traffic. Daniel was right. The cars and trucks didn't run us over, they just acted as if they would. I felt we had survived a major ordeal when we got back into regular street traffic for the rest of the trip home.

The bike, it turned out, took a year of repairs. Dan told me he would help save up the money necessary to replace the missing pedal and to buy some new tires. But each time we fixed one thing and went out for a ride, something else broke before we could get back home. The brakes failed, the chain snapped, spokes fell off the wheel. My dreams of riding around the Bronx as an explorer quickly vanished as each expedition ended with my bicycle breaking down. The bike was junk. If I had been smarter I would have left it right out in front of my father's apartment building. But I couldn't accept the fact that the bicycle was useless. I had come to the realization that this bike was probably going to be it when it came to gifts from my father. I was furious with him that he thought so little of me as to give me something that was obviously broken beyond repair, but somehow throwing my bicycle away came to mean for me throwing my father away—throwing away all those fantasies that he would grow to love me, would come on the block to protect me, that I would get the opportunity to say to somebody, anybody, "My father bought me this."

When it finally happened, that one last breakdown that signaled the end to me, I left the bike lying up against a curb in some strange neighborhood I had ridden to. I refused to be seen walking it back, broken and not working, to Union Avenue one more time. The bike had already cost Daniel and me more than it was worth. As I left it and started the long walk home I thought, "Good riddance." I still saw my father about once every two years, but I never again allowed myself the fantasy that he would learn to love me, protect me, act like a father toward me. He was simply a man who had helped create me and seemed to take no special interest or pride in that fact. In many ways our family was luckier than most who had no fathers because we had a strong mother who did everything she could to make up for the fact that our father was not around and not interested in his children. Yet even though I came to accept that my father would never be there for me, would never see me play varsity football, or basketball, never see me graduate from high school or college, I couldn't help but wonder what it felt like to have a father in your life.

In America today there are more and more children wondering the same thing I wondered as a child—what does it feel like to have a father in your life? The dramatic decline in the presence of fathers in American households is reason for alarm. The decline has been a steady one. What has happened to the American family? Why are so many families headed by young single women? Where are the men? Why aren't men living up to their responsibility to be fathers to their children? This crisis is particularly evident among teenagers. In fact, there is a literal epidemic of unmarried teen mothers in America. There now seems to be solid evidence that the nature of the problem of teenage pregnancy has changed. The facts show that in spite of perceived wisdom, births to girls age fifteen to nineteen were higher in 1960 (89.1 per thousand) and 1970 (68.3) than in 1993 (59.6). What has changed is that teenagers today are much less likely to get married when a girl is pregnant than they used to be. According to Child Trends, Inc., there was a staggering increase in births to unmarried girls in this age group in this country between 1960, when only 15 percent of births to teenagers were nonmarital, and 1993, when 72 percent of these births were nonmarital (Child Trends, Inc., *Facts at a Glance*, 1996).

There are several reasons why households have seen a declining presence of men. Divorce is at an all-time high, for instance, and large numbers of black and Latino men spend a considerable amount of their young adulthood in jail. But these factors don't tell the whole story. I am convinced that the role of fatherhood is a learned one. There is nothing innate about caring for and loving children. As a species, we tend to do what we have been taught to do either by watching others or by formal training. Children learn to be parents by observing how their parents raise them, by watching other parents, and by having short practical learning experiences like baby-sitting. In our culture girls are at a distinct advantage when it comes to learning about parenting. Our cultural norms approve of girls having doll babies and mimicking adult parenting skills. Girls often get the job of taking care of younger siblings. They are usually the first ones we think about when we need a baby-sitter. Girls are rewarded early on for exhibiting behavior that is consistent with mothering. We act as if it is the most natural thing for girls to want to hold the baby, feed the baby, mind the baby.

Our culture has just the opposite expectations of boys. Parents watch for and reinforce early signals of what we have come to accept as signs of masculinity. Boys don't get rewarded for wanting to be around and showing concern for babies. Usually parents discourage boys from playing with dolls or demonstrating any signs of behaviors that we characterize as feminine. Many boys don't ever play at being a parent. As boys grow up they usually learn about fathering, of course, from their own fathers. In homes where there are no fathers, many boys never learn at first hand what fatherhood means; instead they learn what others think it means to be a man. And all too often these two roles are at odds with one another.

When I was growing up in the South Bronx, the older boys spent a lot of time discussing what it meant to be a man. I learned early on that "being a man" on the streets of the Bronx was not an easy thing. Being a man meant being able to "take it." And the "it" they were talking about was everything hard and mean that you had to deal with in growing up poor in America. The first "it" you had to learn to take was pain. Boys learned early on that crying was taboo. It didn't matter whether the pain was caused by physical injury or emotional injury, you were not allowed to cry. The other boys were brutal in their verbal and sometimes physical assault on boys who cried. The names got uglier as you got older. When you were seven or eight years old they called you a "cry-baby" or "mama's boy." By the time you were eleven or twelve the names became crueler—"sissy," "punk," or "faggot."

The other "it" you had to learn to take was being afraid. The older boys and even your peers were always on the lookout for signs of fear. We were taught that any sign of fear was a sign of femininity, and no one thought that was a compliment. All boys at some point had to rise to the challenge "What's the matter, you scared?" The answer could never be "Yes, I'm scared. Who wouldn't be scared to do something like that?" but always, "No, I'm not scared." And you had to prove you were not scared over and over again. This forced you to do things you knew you shouldn't do, things you were afraid to do.

The final thing we were taught en route to manhood was to create an emotional distance between yourself and the rest of the world. We were taught that life contained a series of surprises, all of them nasty, all of them with the express purpose of making you cry, making you scared, breaking you down. We were told we would have to expect a constant barrage of hurt from life—racism, poverty, violence, disappointment, failure, and betrayal. We were taught that the greatest risk of being a poor black man in the ghetto was that you would be robbed of the most sacred thing you had, your manhood. We were preached at over and over again: "Don't ever let anyone or anything take your manhood." And we were taught that men had to harden their hearts against a tough, cold world.

The learn-to-take-it lesson is still being taught to boys, especially poor boys, and this training could not be at greater odds with fathering skills. Imagine a young man who believes that crying is for sissies, that expressing fear is a sign of weakness, that feeling empathy is unmanly—can you imagine that young man caring for a toddler?

We were taught, and many boys are still taught, a way of thinking that can be summed up in two words: "fuck it." If you failed your English class, "fuck it." If the boys from Home Street were after you, "fuck them." If one of your friends stole your girl, "fuck him." If you hurt someone's feelings, that was "too fucking bad." Living life with this as your prevailing philosophy gave you a way to emotionally distance yourself from the hurt, the fear, the pain. And if in our daily choices we disappointed our girlfriends, or teachers, or peers, "fuck it." To care about someone, anyone except your mother, more than yourself was a sign of weakness that could and would be used against you, making it a potential threat to your manhood. Teenage boys today wear their pants so that you can see their underwear: "fuck you." They play their music so loud that you can't hold a conversation: "fuck you." You tell them that if they dress like that and talk like that they will never get a job: "fuck it." And with death from handguns, and AIDS, and generational unemployment, and unhabitable buildings, and no fathers, and broken dreams from poverty creating their reality, I understand them. This is not the kind of social development that creates caring and nurturing fathers.

Add to this equation the fact that boys are taught that sex, not a relationship, is what to want from girls. Add the fact that girls are more willing to have sex with boys after a shorter period of time than was the case in the sixties, that often boys and girls meet and before they even really know one another they are having sex. From many of these short unions children are conceived when there was no intention on the boy's part, nor many times on the girl's, to stay with this partner to raise a family. And you begin to see why so many families start off with two strikes against them.

Often infidelity further weakens this poor foundation. The boy's feelings for the baby are usually determined by his feelings for the baby's mother. If he wants to stay with her, he will accept a more traditional role as father. But if he doesn't, or if he still wants to see and sleep with other girls as well, he feels no real connection with the developing fetus, and the baby often becomes just a side issue in his life. No real bond is formed with his child, and over time he feels no connection, no love.

To deal forcefully with the issue of fatherhood in America we need to make a conscientious effort to see that all boys have a real and tangible understanding of what it means to be a father. We cannot allow boys to continue to think of the act of sex as pure recreation that carries no consequences. The message that babies need mothers *and fathers* has to be delivered more powerfully. The act of fathering a child must take on the same prominence as mothering a child. The issues of responsibility and the financial and emotional support of children must become part of the learning of every adolescent boy. And we need to connect boys to men. Men who can spend time fathering and teaching boys how to be good fathers. Many more of us need to commit to being such men and to having a place in the lives of boys from a very early age.

One of the things that we as a society must do right away is reconnect the fact of fatherhood with being financially responsible for the child. While this country has spent a great deal of time and effort coming up with a welfare reform plan that puts welfare mothers to work, we have not examined the fact that often the fathers of these children are not working and need jobs. How is it that we hold the mother responsible for working and not the father? This is another clear example of how we devalue the role of fathers in raising children. How do we teach that the responsibility of raising children is equally shared by mother and father when we insist that only one, the mother, must work to support the child?

One of the things we do at Rheedlen is to make sure our programs have caring and nurturing men in them, both young and old, so that our boys and girls understand that men play a role in bringing up children. Our boys see men holding children's hands, wiping their tears away, reading them stories. So even if they don't have a father at home, they grow up knowing how normal it is for men to show concern, love, and tenderness for children. Many of the little boys in our programs see the young men who work for Rheedlen—men who don't curse, use drugs, drink, or intimidate children—as role models, and they want to be like them. We think every boy needs the experience of being around such men, so that he has concrete examples of how men care for and nurture children. The problem of fathering will only be solved when we connect boys to men in relationships that last over time and give boys the opportunity to develop a fuller sense of what it really means to be a man.

Sex

THE FIRST TIME I realized that maybe I was behind the curve on discussing sex with my children was thirteen years ago, when my daughter Melina and my son Jerry were watching John Travolta in *Saturday Night Fever* on cable television. My daughter was thirteen at the time and my son eleven. I'd been to the store and walked into the house just as two boys on the screen were talking about how one had gotten a "blow job" from a girl.

I stood in the doorway with my mouth open. I had watched this movie several times. I thought the music was great and the story seemed fairly tame to me, so I thought nothing of it when my children had asked if they could watch it.

"Turn that off!" I yelled, causing both my children to startle. They looked at me uncomprehending.

"Turn that off! Didn't you hear me? Turn that off right now! Who told you you could watch stuff like this?"

"You did, Daddy," my daughter said as she got up to turn the television off. She looked at her brother as she walked back to her chair as if to say, Has he completely lost his mind?

"Well, that was before I realized it was a dirty movie," I sputtered.

"It's been on all week, Daddy. We've watched it before. What's the big deal?"

Suddenly I was relieved. They didn't know. I felt so foolish. They didn't know what a blow job was. They probably thought she was fixing his hair or something. Should I tell them what I was upset about? If I identified "blow job" as the problem, they'd want to know what the words meant. I decided to tell them why I was upset, but not to explain more than I had to.

"They used some words just now that I don't like. I was upset because you two were watching and they were using what I would call bad language."

"What words, Daddy?" my son asked.

"Er . . . well . . . they used the word . . . the word 'blow job.' "

"Oh, *that*," my daughter said dismissively.

" 'Oh, *that*.' What do you mean, 'Oh, *that*'?" I asked with alarm.

"Nothing. I mean, so what?"

"So what? Do you know what that means?" I asked, getting upset all over again.

"Oh, Daddy," Melina said, using the same tone she does whenever she thinks I'm overreacting in some old-fashioned adult way.

I turned to my son. "And you? Do you know what that means?"

Jerry put his head between his hands and started giggling. He knew. I was shocked. I retreated into the kitchen and tried to compose myself. My children were too young to be so blasé about oral sex. Where had they heard about that? I realized my children were being exposed to much more explicit sexual information than I had realized. Where was it coming from? I began to watch television more closely, and, not surprisingly, much of what they wanted to watch had more explicit sex and violence than I had realized. I made it a habit from that point on to look at shows on television not from my vantage point as an adult, but from the vantage point of a child. After that, there were many shows my children were told they could not watch.

But my struggles as a father in the early eighties are tame in comparison to what faces parents today. Explicit sex in the movies, in videos, and on CDs and tapes has become literally unavoidable. In every urban area huge billboards show men in underwear striking poses that blatantly suggest sex. Women clad in their underwear float by on the sides of buses and cause barely an eyebrow to raise. Sex is used to sell everything to everyone, including to young people. This change in how and what children learn about sex has been so sudden and dramatic that it's hard for any of us to understand what it means for our children's sense of themselves. One thing is for sure: boys have always been particularly avid consumers of whatever sexual information is available.

In the fifties, sex for a twelve-year-old consisted of dirty words scrawled on a bathroom wall. We thought it daring and bold if another child had the audacity to write *P-U-S-S-Y* in the street with chalk. We had plenty of interest in and virtually no knowledge of what sex really consisted of. Still, the conversations we held on the stoop, or standing on the corner, increasingly had to do with sex as we approached adolescence. The older boys were our only source of information on sex, but they were often maddeningly unhelpful.

We'd be sitting near the older boys, and one would say, "Man, look at Josephine. She's looking fine. Sure would like to have a piece of that. Whaddabout you, Geoff? You want some of that?"

"Yeah . . . I mean, sure I want some." Laughter.

"Hey, Junior, you hear little Geoff? He want some of Josephine. Boy, you wouldn't know what to do with no real girl like that. Your little dick couldn't even fit in." More laughter.

"Yes it would, man. Yes it would. It ain't small, man. It's big. Real big."

"Okay, Geoff. What would you do? Huh? If you had Josephine in the bed, man, what would you do? You wouldn't even know where to put it."

"Yes I would too. I know where."

"Where? Go on, tell me. Where?"

"I . . . uh, uh . . . I would put it—you know—I would put it in."

"In what? In what?"

"You know . . . in there. I would put it in."

"He can't even say it. Little Geoff, it's called a pussy. And you know what? If a little nigger like you put your little dick in a big pussy like that, she'd grab it with her pussy, and you'd be stuck. Stuck, man. Just like a dog in the street. Somebody have to come in and throw cold water on you like you have to do a dog. That's why you can't fuck with no big girl pussy like that, man. You hear me?"

I was stunned. I had seen dogs stuck together in the act of sex before. It certainly didn't look like any fun. And now to find out that the same thing could happen to me. I knew he was right. It *was* little. And on Union Avenue having a "little dick" was like being cursed. I used to pray to God to make mine grow before any of the older boys saw it. And now I find out that because mine is little, I could end up being stuck like a dog, caught until somebody came with a pot of cold water. I trembled with the fear that my mother would find me like that. In the bed with a girl, calling for help. Would she give me a beating? Maybe she would just leave me there, stuck, and say, "Now you've learned your lesson." I decided if I ever got a girl to give me some I would have my brother Dan stand by with a pot of cold water just in case. It had to be Dan. My brother John was too big a tease; he would agree to do it, then at the last minute when I was stuck and needed him he wouldn't throw the water on us, he'd run and get all the guys and bring them in to laugh at me. Naw, I thought, it definitely had to be Dan.

I began to wonder if it was worth it. This pussy thing sounded kind of dangerous. I mean, how good could it be? And just how did you do it, anyway? According to the older guys, some guys could really do it, and some guys couldn't do it at all. What was there to do? And why was it so bad if you had never done it? I mean, you were in real trouble if you were one of the older guys and you had never done it. They said you were afraid of it, and laughed. Would I ever do it?

Each day, the issue of "getting some" seemed to grow in importance. By the time I was thirteen I was sure my friend Ned and I were the only boys our age who hadn't gotten any. By that time we both had girlfriends and we had kissed them. But the kissing we did was with a closed mouth, and while we got all hot and bothered we had no idea what came next. The pressure to "do it" from the other boys became too much. The guys were unrelenting with their questions, especially Tommy. I didn't want to lie but I felt I had no choice.

"Hey, Geoff. You still going out with Brenda?"

"Yeah, we going out."

"Well?"

"Well what?"

"You know. Did she let you do it?"

"Naw, man. Almost, you know. But not yet."

"Did she let you feel her titties?"

"Why you wanna know? That's between me and her."

"I bet you didn't even cop a feel. Did ya?"

"Aw man, shut up. She let me cop a feel, man. What you talking about? You go out with Barbara—did *you* get some, Mr. Romeo?"

"Yeah, I got it." With that one pronouncement all of our attention was riveted on Tommy. He had done it. We were in awe.

"You lying, man, you didn't do it. She ain't gonna let you do it to her."

"Nigger, are you crazy? I did it. I fucked her."

Our attention was totally focused on Tommy. Alan asked, "You fucked her? How was it, man? Was it good?"

"Yeah, man, it was real good. But she didn't know how to do it too good. I had to show her."

"Did you hump her or did you just put it in?"

"Man, I humped her. I humped her for hours, man. She was lovin' it. I was tearin' it up, man. She was screaming and everything."

Then the question that was on everyone's mind: "Did you come, man?"

"Huh?"

"Did you *come*? You said you was fucking her for hours—did you come or what? Nigger ain't even come. I bet he's lying."

"What the fuck you talking about? I came, man. I came for about fifteen or twenty minutes. I came all over the place, man. I came so much, man, we had to get the mop bucket because it wouldn't stop."

We were all captivated by Tommy's story. We were truly impressed. I thought to myself, I guess if I ever get some I better tell my brother Dan not to leave with the pot after he throws the cold water on me, I might need it for all the come. I wondered if the big pot would be big enough. Better get the mop bucket like Tommy just to be safe. I was a little bigger than Tommy so maybe even the mop bucket wouldn't be big enough. This pussy thing was becoming a bigger headache every day.

And the boys never stopped asking if I had gotten any yet. Every day another one of them confessed that he had finally gotten some. And it was good. And he humped it for hours. And he tore it up. With each confession came slapping on the back and general celebration: someone else had finally gotten it, had joined the club. My problem was that neither Brenda nor I were contemplating sex. I wasn't ready for something quite that complicated. You needed people with water standing by, there was this big mess to deal with. The pressure finally got to me, though, and the day came when I had to tell the boys I had done it.

"Geoff, you done it yet or no? Boy, you ain't gonna never get none. Whatssamatter, you scared of it?"

"I got it last night."

"You got it? You really got it? You fucked Brenda?"

"Yeah, man. I was up her house and her mother and father went out and she let me do it."

"Did you tear it up?"

"Aw man, did I? I took off her clothes and we did it in her bed. I was doing it, man. I did it so hard the bed broke down."

"You broke the bed down? What did you do then?"

"We just kept doing it, man. I didn't care. It took me half an hour to fix the bed back. Her mother came back just as I finished. I almost got caught." I could see rapt attention in their faces. They believed me.

Tommy asked the question on everyone's mind. "Did she try to grab you with it? Did you get stuck?"

"She tried, man, but I was too strong. It took all my strength to get out, man. I was almost stuck. I was scared, man." With that there was a solemn nodding of heads, the wise men of experience celebrating another one of the boys who had escaped the infamous grabbing pussy.

Brenda and I didn't stay boyfriend and girlfriend for too long after I told the lie that we'd had sex together. And not having a girlfriend took the pressure off of me to make up more lies about sex. Then something seemed to change within me. I had no idea where it came from, but it was one of the most powerful changes I had ever experienced. I can remember the evening like it was yesterday. It was summer, and I was walking in the Bronx past the

Saint Mary's projects, which in those days were kept clean and safe. The music "A Fork in the Road," sung by Smokey Robinson, drifted over the warm summer night like a breeze. I had heard the song before, but it had never sounded like it did that evening. I knew I was away from my block, in unfamiliar territory, and that trouble could be around any corner, but I was drawn to the music like the proverbial moth to a flame.

The song was coming from a recreational center packed with teenagers. Smokey was singing, "Oh why / couldn't I see the sign. / Before I / left my love behind / at the fork in the road . . ." I gawked through a window, completely mesmerized. The teenagers were dancing, boys' arms wrapped around girls, girls' heads tucked into the shoulders of boys, swaying to the music, oblivious to all else on a summer's night. The music died down, the couples broke apart, and I started for the door. I had to get inside. Listening to that song and watching those kids seemed to open up something inside me, and a need to be close to the girls and possibly hold one in my arms surged in me like never before.

I walked toward the front door of the center in a trance. I was halfway there before I noticed the group of boys hanging around outside. They were all well dressed and looking directly at me. They could tell I didn't belong: this party was for boys who dressed in jackets and girls in frilly dresses. I looked down at my sneakers and dungarees, then back at the boys. I realized from the looks I was getting that there was no way I was getting into that dance without a fight. The boys started toward me and my hand instinctively went into my right pants pocket where I carried my knife. I wasn't afraid of them. Just like they could take one look at me and tell I was a poor boy from the ghetto, I could look at them and tell they were the closest thing we had to middle-class boys in our neighborhood. They didn't really want to tangle with someone like me. They stopped and I stopped with my finger resting on my knife in my pocket. It was a standoff. I turned and walked away with the sound of Smokey Robinson still drifting to my ears. I'd never felt so lonely in my life. Somewhere boys and girls were holding one another, sharing a moment of tenderness, and I was alone walking the streets of the South Bronx.

The vision of those lovely girls in their party dresses was burned into my mind. There was a hunger deep inside me, and I thought it was my hunger alone. It didn't take me long, though, to find out that I wasn't the only one who had discovered dances. That summer all the boys my age began to talk about going to parties. We were essentially divided into two groups, those who had gone to at least one party and those who hadn't. I was in the second group. It wasn't that I didn't want to go to the parties. But I had to be upstairs by nine P.M., and that was the earliest any of these parties even got started. More importantly, I didn't know how to dance, an impediment almost as crippling as not wearing Converse sneakers.

I was able to make up excuses about why I wasn't at this or that party for most of the summer, but the other boys didn't make it easy. In the evenings, once we had all come back downstairs from dinner, the conversation would turn to girls and the party on Friday or Saturday night. Alan, Tommy, Neddy, and David all lived on Union Avenue. We would all sit on the stoop after dinner and sooner or later the subject would come up. Tommy usually knew all about parties because he had an older brother and sister.

"You know there's a party on Tinton Avenue Friday night. You guys coming?" he'd ask.

"Yeah, I might go as long as it's not lame," Dave might say. "I mean, if nothing's happening I'm outta there. What about you, Geoff? You going?"

"Aw, I don't know. It probably won't be no big deal. I'm waiting for a really good party."

Then Alan would give it to us. "You know your momma won't let you stay out at night to go to no party. Who you tryin' to fool? You gotta be in the house before dark."

This brought protest from everyone. We all claimed we could stay out as long as we wanted. We all lied. I knew everyone's parents, and while some households were more chaotic than others, we all had fairly early curfews. The truth was, even if my curfew had allowed partygoing, I was scared. As much as I wanted to go because girls would be there, I was afraid the other boys on the block would see I couldn't dance. Typically, after one of the boys my age finagled his way to stay out late enough to go to a party, the next day he caught hell from the older boys on the block.

"Did you see Tommy last night, trying to dance? He can't dance worth shit. He can't even grind." At this everyone would laugh. I laughed too, even though I didn't know what they were talking about. In my laughter I was hoping to blend in, to not draw attention to myself, but it didn't work.

"Geoff, you know how to grind?"

"Sure I do. Everybody knows how to do that," I lied, wondering what a grind was.

"Quit lying, nigger. You ain't even been to a party before. You ain't never grind before."

"Get the fuck out of here, man. I did so. You don't know what you talking about. You the one don't know how to grind." I could feel myself getting in over my head.

"Fucking liar. What party you ever been to? Huh? Tommy may not know how to grind but at least he goes to parties. He's down. You scared of girls, Geoff? That why you don't come with us? Or your momma won't let you stay out past dark? Your momma still treating you like a baby?"

"Leave my fucking mother out of this shit or I'll kick your fucking ass. All right. Fuck you, man. I can go to a party if I want to. I was gonna go to the one on Tinton Avenue, but you know I had that beef with Rory, and I didn't want to start no static. But that's none of your fucking business. Why don't you learn to mind your fucking business 'fore I make you?"

"Why you getting all mad and shit? Why you wanna start a fight? I just said you ain't never been to a party. It's true. Whatssamatta? You can dish it out but you can't take it?"

"Naw, man. Just don't say nothing 'bout my mother, that's all. I didn't say nothing about your mother. And you know I could say a lot of shit about your mother if I wanted to."

"Aw c'mon, Geoff. Why you wanna be like that? See, you always wanna start something. Okay, forget it. But you know there's a party right on the block Saturday. It's gonna be right across the street from your building. The boys from Tinton won't be coming on our block. You coming?"

I was trapped. What could I say? "Of course I'm coming. Why wouldn't I come? Who's gonna be there?"

We talked about which boys and girls were coming and I acted as if going to a party was an everyday event in my life. The problem was I didn't know if I could go, or what I would do once I got there.

It was not going to be easy convincing my mother, but I did have a couple of things in my favor. The party was directly across the street from my building. My mother would know where I was and who I was with. Still, it wasn't easy to convince her. After a great deal of pleading and promising, I was granted permission to stay out until eleven P.M. One problem down. Now I had to find out what this dance called the grind was. I went to find Tommy and Alan, who were the only ones of us who had actually gone to a party. They laughed at me, smug in their knowledge. Alan explained, "To grind with a girl you ask her to dance off of a slow record. Then you wrap both your arms around her like in a bear hug, you put one of your legs between hers, and you grind up against her."

My mouth fell open. I couldn't believe it. I asked, "And they just let you do that? Girls, I mean. They just let you grind on them?"

"Yeah, stupid. They like it."

I was too intrigued to worry about the name calling. "How do you get them to grind with you?"

"You just go up to them and say, 'Do you want to dance?' and they say yes, and that's it."

My head was swimming. I couldn't believe girls would let you do that, much less like it. I needed more information. "So how do you do it? I mean, how does it go?"

Alan explained. "First you put one leg between their legs, then on the beat you slide your leg between theirs, and on the next beat they slide their leg between yours. Like this."

Alan pretended he had both arms tightly around a girl. His legs slid back and forth and his hips ground against thin air as he moved to an imaginary slow song. We all stared, trying to memorize every move. For the next few days I practiced grinding in the bathroom mirror. It really was quite simple in comparison with some of the fast dances I was trying to learn, which took real coordination and a good deal of stamina. I knew I could never master the mashed potatoes in time for the party. Your feet had to slide beneath you in opposite directions, your fingers popping to the beat, your body twisting this way and that. It was just too hard to do all of that and not miss a beat. But grinding—I thought I could master this by Saturday night.

The big night arrived, but my first disappointment of the evening came early. Nobody wanted to go to the party before ten P.M. I couldn't believe it, I had to be home by eleven. After what seemed to be a lifetime, the guys thought enough time had passed and we went upstairs to the party. The first thing that struck me was how dark it was. The red bulb in the ceiling fixture gave off just enough light to see. I squinted as I made my way around the room, saying hi to all of my friends so they would all be sure to know I had come to the party. Most of the songs were fast songs and I stood by the wall with other boys who couldn't dance, trying to act as if I *could* but chose not to. A slow song came on and I watched with amazement as boys asked girls to dance and everyone began to grind. Alan was right, the girls seemed to be enjoying themselves just as much as the boys. I waited for my opportunity. There were several fast songs, then another slow one. I started walking over to a girl I had my eye on. Another boy got there first. I spotted another girl, but a boy grabbed her hand just as I approached. I turned to find another partner. Too late. Everyone was already dancing. Feeling somewhat foolish, I went back to the wall to watch and wait.

At the next slow song I sprang off the wall, grabbed the closest girl, and said, "Would you like to dance?" She looked at me, rolled her eyes, and, sucking her teeth, said, "No." Even as she said no, one of the older boys grabbed her hand and enfolded her in his arms. I couldn't move. I was sure everyone had seen me get rejected. Alan had never told me the girl might say no. I stumbled back to the wall and stayed there, all my old insecurities flooding back. I knew I had been rejected because I didn't have nice clothes, or a caesar haircut (hair cut low and rounded at the front). The boys came over one by one, asking me if I was ever going to dance. I kept saying, "Yeah, in a minute. Once my song comes on." Their looks showed they weren't buying it.

This dance was becoming a nightmare. Tomorrow all the guys would be talking about how I was a wallflower all night and didn't dance. My time was running out. It was already eleven and I should be leaving to be home on time. I was in a panic about what to do. Just then someone put on Smokey Robinson's "A Fork in the Road" and almost as one, all of the boys got off the wall and started moving toward the girls. I moved as if drawn by a magnet. Smokey's plaintive voice was too much for even my adolescent shyness. The boys were swarming over by the girls and it was clear I wasn't the only one who thought Smokey was talking to me, about how I felt, understanding something about us that we didn't know until he sang it. I saw her. She was on the wall in a red dress. Several boys walked right by her to ask other girls to dance. She was like me, not the best looking, not the best dressed. I dodged my way through the crowd of boys and girls already dancing, wanting to get there quickly but not wanting to seem desperate. I asked her, "Would you like to dance?" She smiled and came into my arms.

I had never felt anything so soft and so warm in my life. I pressed my pelvis tentatively against hers, she pressed back harder. I held her a little tighter, she held even tighter. We moved as one until something began to happen that I hadn't thought to ask Alan about. It had never occurred to me that such close physical contact, with all of that grinding, might cause an erection. My God, what would she think? Would she just walk away from me there on the dance floor? I tried to will it down. But I could feel it sliding up my leg, becoming larger and more insistent. She couldn't help but rub up against it. I held my breath. She felt it and to my surprise she opened her legs so that she could grind up against it. I was in heaven. I began to dip down so that my hardness would rub right between her legs. I looked around me and saw that I wasn't the only one who was rocking and dipping. Indeed the whole room seemed to be doing the same thing. I closed my eyes and knew I was in love.

When the record ended I was ready to ask this wonderful girl to be my girlfriend. I felt that we had really gotten to know one another during the dance, even though we hadn't exactly said anything to one another. As I opened my mouth to ask her to be mine, she said, "Thank you," turned away, and left. How could she leave? I know she had to feel it, the attraction, the closeness, that we were made for each other. Another slow song came on and I thanked my lucky stars for two in a row. I went to ask my soul-mate for another dance, but another boy beat me to it. She smiled at him and held him the same way she had held me. He began to grind with her and she began to grind back. I realized I had just learned an important lesson about grinding: it didn't mean a thing. I eased my way to the door. Several of my friends gave me a pat on the back, they had seen me in action. There would be no jokes about Geoff not dancing at the party. He could grind with the best of them. I left happy but confused. How could something so intimate be so meaningless? That night I went to sleep and dreamed about holding hands and whispering into the ear of a girl in a red dress.

The experience of grinding with the girl in the red dress changed me. I knew that I wanted to be with girls. I knew that I wanted to hold them and caress them and soon I knew that I wanted to have sex with them.

In 1963, though, there was little chance of that happening. I had to be content with Friday and Saturday night parties where you could grind with a few girls and maybe if you were really lucky you could "cop a feel." My friends and I wanted sex, all right, it was just much harder to come by in the early sixties.

Why? For one thing, there were more adults around all the time. To have sex you needed a willing partner, but also a place where you could be alone for a period of time. In my neighbor-hood there was nearly always a parent, usually a mother, at home, but if not there'd be a grandmother or an aunt, or a made-to-be-responsible older sibling—or at the least a very vigilant neighbor looking out the window or down the hall. Today, with so many couples working, and so many single mothers working, too many teens have apartments and homes where they can be alone and fairly sure no one is going to interrupt them.

Another reason more teens engage in sex at an earlier age is that sexually explicit materials are right in their face all the time. After constant exposure over and over again to pictures, story lines, and graphic images of a sexual nature, boys often come to wrongly believe that they really know all there is to know about sex. The awkwardness and uncertainty of youth once prevented many boys from getting a false sense of confidence regarding sex. I saw my first picture of a nude woman when I was in the sixth grade; it nearly caused a riot in the schoolyard as boys pushed and shoved, trying to get a look at the playing card with the naked woman that some boy had snuck from his home. Today youth are bombarded with knowledge and images of sex that contain enough information that boys think they can simply act out what they've seen on television or in the movies.

Even in a book about boys, it bears saying that one of the most dramatic changes I've noticed in regard to relationships and early sexual experiences between children has occurred with girls. The sexual revolution of the late sixties and early seventies seems to me to have had less to do with boys and men and more to do with girls and women. As many of us remember, there used to be great pressure put on girls to not engage in sex or in any type of behavior that could be construed as openly sexual. A girl had a "reputation," and just being seen with the wrong type of boy could "ruin" it. Most young girls didn't curse in the open, didn't openly drink or use drugs, were not allowed out at night (except maybe on their front stoop), and never let on in public that they had sexual feelings. If a girl did have sex with a boy it was considered a big secret; any inkling that sex had taken place would fuel the rumors that so-and-so had "done it." This was considered very big news when I was in junior high school and fear of the stigma involved certainly put the brakes on many a girl's unbridled passion. There was an even greater taboo against any girl having multiple partners or giving the impression that she liked sex as much as boys did. Both boys and girls considered any girl who had more than one sexual liaison in junior high school a "ho," as we used to say. Boys wanted to be with such a girl only for sex, but never to be seen with her, and other girls were afraid to be friends with her lest their own reputations be sullied by association.

Today girls, like boys, are constantly getting messages via the media and social norms that suggest that they can be much more open about their own sexuality, and this includes the freedom to have multiple sexual partners without the taboos that once existed. While this has removed a lot of the unfair stigma placed on girls who have sex and has helped eliminate the double standard that favored males, we are now in a situation where there are few social constraints and almost no stigma on very young adolescents having sex.

The alarming rate of consumption of alcohol and other drugs by teenagers (more on this later) also contributes to earlier and more frequent sex. If they are high or drunk, children are less likely to care about the warnings that their parents and teachers have issued about risky behaviors.

I wanted sex at twelve and thirteen, but the closest I came to it was slow dancing under a red light. For years my friends and I chased those red lights all over the Bronx, paying our quarters to get inside the warm confines of a "grind me up." I would be five or six years older before I had sex with a girl, and even then, finding a place and opportunity proved difficult. If back at the age of twelve or thirteen we had known girls who were willing, I know what would have happened: sex, lots of it and all the time. The reason more of us didn't become teen parents had little to do with values about family and marriage. We simply didn't know a lot about sex and couldn't find willing partners.

But the sexual revolution was right around the corner. Part of the aftermath of that revolution is a weakened nuclear family with fewer fathers present in the household and many only marginally involved with their children's lives. We also have an advertising and media establishment that is emboldened to put ever more sexual titillation out across our airwaves, often targeted at our children. We have created a culture for boys that on the one hand makes it too easy for them to become fathers and, on the other, teaches them nothing about what fatherhood means.

Drugs

I'VE WRITTEN that there's much about the way we bring up boys that conspires to make them into risk takers. Growing up, my friends and I took risks all the time. We jumped off rooftops, climbed over barbed-wire fences, had rock fights. Later we accepted the folklore that being a man meant being able to "hold your liquor," and we became fascinated with getting high. We knew that to reach some of these highs you had to take risks, but for us risk taking had already become a way of life.

This conditioning serves to break down any barriers between boys and drug use. And there are other messages sent by parents and other adults in authority that surround and complicate boys' use of drugs and alcohol. The adults I grew up with tended to classify all drugs as equally debilitating, equally addictive. But on the streets we learned different. We could see the varied effects that hard drugs like heroin and cocaine and soft drugs like marijuana had on people. Our restricted sense of cause and effect, limited by our young person's sense of time, hampered our ability to make logical deductions about drug use. We saw that while over what passed for a long period of time in a boy's mind (six months or a year) those who smoked pot seemed just fine, those on heroin became junkies. We knew lots of kids who smoked pot and had not gone on to use harder drugs, so we thought we had good reason to reject most of what our parents and teachers told us about it. We especially scoffed at adults who told us marijuana was a terrible drug and said nothing about alcohol, especially when we could see how alcohol had destroyed so many men and women on the block who were known drunks.

Parents today are sending different but often equally ineffective messages regarding drug use. Many of us who are part of the baby-boomer generation have had plenty of firsthand experience with a variety of drugs. We might feel dishonest preaching in absolute terms about the ills of something that we did ourselves as teenagers. Most adults from my generation have stopped using drugs, but there are some who must deal with the conflict of using them even when their children become teenagers and might well be doing the same thing. We know better than to repeat the mistakes of our parents by ranting and raving about the evils of marijuana. But I fear that what has occurred because of our timidity on the drug issue is that we have far too often just said nothing. We have not given our children a clear message about where we stand on drug use and why. This might feel like a difficult thing to do with any honesty unless we admit to our own drug use. It's not just past drug use that needs to be discussed— parents should remember that if they smoke or drink at home, and never talk about how or why they do, their children barely stand a chance of doing otherwise.

My friends and I started experimenting with drugs when we were in junior high school. We began with what most kids begin with today, alcohol and tobacco. We were all going through puberty, interested in sports, girls, and fitting in. One boy we knew started to drink at twelve, and it was natural on Union Avenue that most of us would follow by the time we were thirteen or fourteen. All the boys on the block drank before their fifteenth birthday. It was the same with smoking cigarettes; most of us wanted to do it, only a few didn't. For us, drinking was a way to belong and an activity in and of itself. For boys with nothing to do, drinking was doing something. Despite what our parents told us, drinking was fun, and to us it seemed safe.

By the time we began drinking, many of us had already been smoking for a while. Smoking cigarettes for most of us was the first time we had defied our parents and society in general. We were all told we were not allowed to smoke. This was during the early sixties, and much of what we know now about the dangers of cigarettes was not understood by the general public. Still, our parents, most of whom smoked, told us we had to wait until we were grown before we could smoke. Many of us asked our parents why they smoked. And the answers they gave us were "It relaxes me," or "I just enjoy it." The fact that our parents didn't know to say to us, "This is a terrible habit that I can't quit, and it's not good for me," ensured that we would all start smoking cigarettes sooner or later. The power of parents as role models to their children can be easily understood by remembering how many of us learned how to smoke because our parents did.

My mother was adamant that my brothers and I couldn't smoke, and we were just as determined to learn how. Experimenting with cigarettes was easy because she smoked, and we could find cigarette butts in the ashtray. It was with one of these stale, half-smoked cigarettes that I first began. My brother and I straightened out the crushed cigarette and lit it. We puffed on the stub without inhaling. I remember thinking, "This isn't so hard." We put the cigarette between our fingers as we had seen so many grownups do. We parodied the way adults walked and talked when they smoked. And it was great fun.

We thought we knew how to smoke until a friend who was a little older saw us in the hallway and rudely informed us that what we were doing was "kiddie stuff." That you weren't really smoking until you inhaled. So we set about trying to master inhaling. Young and healthy lungs respond reflexively. The first time I inhaled tobacco smoke, I choked and gagged. If there is a clearer signal from your body that something is bad for it, I don't know what it is. I remember thinking I would never really learn how to smoke. But so powerful was the desire to look grownup, to be like grownups, that even though I coughed and choked, I managed to get enough smoke into my lungs to exhale. In a matter of a week or two I had managed to repress my body's own warning signals and had become a cigarette smoker.

Millions of children began using drugs just as I did. Whether we like it or not, the first drug pushers our children come in contact with are often their parents—us. When we look forward to a drink, we teach them that drugs are fun, a part of life; when we smoke cigarettes around them, we show them exactly how to use a drug. When we smoke cigarettes, drink, smoke marijuana, or use other drugs (including prescription drugs) and leave them in the house, thinking our children won't find them or use them, all too often they do. Children are programmed to learn from adults; that's how our species has survived and prospered. If we smoke, our children will more than likely smoke; if we drink, our children will drink. And while we might have figured out our limits, and which drugs we can use safely and which we must avoid, we can't expect the same sophistication from a thirteen-year-old.

When I was a teenager, many of our parents drank alcohol but did not know we drank. Hiding our drinking from our parents was the responsibility of the group. Right before it was time for us to go home, we would chew gum or suck on mints to cover the alcohol on our breath. We would walk an obviously intoxicated kid in fresh air or not allow him to go home until his head cleared. Many of us became experts at hiding our drinking and smoking from our parents. While many of the older boys drank beer out of paper cups in the afternoon, we did not. Our drinking was confined to the evening, and we drank cheap wine.

The most expensive wine we drank cost fifty cents for a pint and was sold chilled by local liquor stores. The wines were named Gypsy Rose, Thunderbird, and Swiss Up. Custom dictated that when you screwed off the top of the bottle (none of us drank wine that came with a cork), you poured a small amount on the sidewalk. This was for the "boys upstate," those doing time in some upstate reformatory school. Each boy rubbed the top of the wine bottle with an open hand, to erase germs left over from the last drinker, then opened his mouth, leaned back his head, and literally poured the wine into his mouth without his lips touching the bottle.

Each guzzle of wine was followed by watering eyes, grimaces, head shaking, and foot stomping, all in acknowledgment of the potency of the alcohol. This was pure rotgut. There was no pretense that this was sipping wine, with a delicate bouquet and flavor to be enjoyed. This was wine created for only one reason—to intoxicate. We poured it down our throats because there was no way you could sip it and do anything but spit it out. We learned to drink to get high, plain and simple. Sooner or later all the boys had to make a choice: be part of the group and drink wine on Friday and Saturday nights or be considered a "lame," a "square." And no matter how much some boys feared drinking wine, or knew that it was wrong, nearly all succumbed to the pressure. Slowly but surely we all learned to drink wine and we learned to like it, and many of the boys on Union Avenue were on their way to destroying their lives.

In the sixties there were plenty of warnings from adults that using marijuana might lead to harder drugs. But to boys like us, boys who by fifteen were already smoking cigarettes and drinking, who had passed the hurdle of engaging in behaviors that were illegal and frowned on by our parents, these warnings meant little. Our parents had warned us that smoking cigarettes and drinking were not good for us, but as far as we could tell these things had no lasting effect on us, physically or mentally.

Years later I would sometimes talk to my friends about why they did or didn't use "hard" drugs. I was surprised by what my friends who became addicted told me about the beginnings of their drug use. They tried heroin, which was the drug of choice for many of the boys on the block (cocaine was not to become a scourge in poor communities for another twenty-five years), and they were scared the first time or two. But nothing happened. They didn't crave the drug, it had no lasting effect on their bodies; all in all it seemed fairly benign. The fact that for them the drug seemed to have no strong allure is what allowed so many to become addicted. They each decided that, unlike everybody else, they and their friends were somehow immune to the addictive quality of the drug, that they could use it once or twice on weekends without getting "strung out." They thought that for them heroin was just like smoking or drinking, a thing your parents told you was terrible for you but that turned out to be not all that bad.

There were several reasons I never tried heroin. The first was that Mike, an older boy who'd become my role model, explained to me early on all about heroin, using live educational aids that made an impression. He would point out all the older guys in the neighborhood who were using heroin and talk about what stage they had reached in their addiction. Mike would walk over to those he knew to be sniffing heroin and challenge them on their drug use. They would all say the same thing: "C'mon, Mike, you know me. I can handle that shit. I ain't gonna shoot it like those other guys. I ain't stupid." Mike would admonish them about who they were hanging out with and how they were going to "fuck up" their lives. They would all promise Mike they wouldn't do heroin anymore. They all would be lying.

At the next stage were those boys who were "skin popping," injecting heroin under their skin but not directly into their veins. When they saw Mike coming they would all get nervous. They could guess what was coming. They could no longer pretend that they were on their way to quitting; they knew they were on their way to becoming junkies. Their response to Mike would always be, "Listen, Mike. I'm quitting, man. I had enough. I ain't no junkie or nothing. Watch, you'll see. I'm gonna be straight." It was usually a very few months before those boys moved into the next group, those who mainlined drugs.

Once boys started shooting heroin into their veins their attitude changed. They no longer denied their drug use, they admitted they did it and said they liked it. Their only disclaimer was they weren't "strung out." Mike considered these guys to be usually past the borderline of salvation, on their way down a one-way street to disaster.

Even as Mike was working on me, I saw something that convinced me that heroin was not for me. There was a basement apartment that a couple of the older guys lived in from time to time that also served as the neighborhood hangout when the weather got cold. We called the apartment "the cut." Entrance was by invitation only. Because I'd become good friends with Mike, I was one of the few young boys allowed. Things happened in the cut; it seemed to me a place of great mystery and secrets.

The older boys told stories there that they never told on the streets. It was a place to drink, to smoke marijuana, or on rare occasions to bring a girl for sex. I loved being able to go to the cut. You never knew what you would find going on in there. But mostly we went to the cut to drink our wine before heading out to a party to grind with girls.

On this particular Friday night I was in the cut with my friend Tommy. The cut had an old beat-up record player and we had about three records we would play over and over. Tommy and I were sharing a "corner" of Gypsy Rose wine we had begged from one of the older boys. There wasn't a lot of wine left in the bottle, but that was the good thing about Gypsy Rose, you didn't need much. We had both just taken a drink and were busy singing along with Smokey Robinson, pretending the bottle was our microphone. We were so intent on our harmonizing we barely noticed Jamie and Freddie when they came in. They completely ignored us and began to pull things out of their pockets with an intensity that stopped Tommy and me in mid-chorus.

Jamie took charge; it was obvious he was the pro. "You get the works set up and I'll make the cooker."

With that, Jamie began to dig the cork out of a bottle cap with a small knife. After he got all the cork out and washed the cap, he produced a small glassine envelope from his pocket. Tommy and I couldn't believe what we knew was about to happen. There was an unwritten rule that older guys didn't shoot up in front of young boys like us, but nobody else was in the cut at that moment and these two clearly didn't care if we watched. They put a small amount of water in the bottle cap and then the heroin, then heated the heroin and water with a lit match until Jamie pronounced it ready.

By the time the heroin began to cook the two older boys acted if they were completely oblivious to our presence. Their whole attention was on the drugs. Jamie told Freddie to roll up his sleeve. He took off his belt, wrapped it around Freddie's upper arm, and pulled it tight until the veins in Freddie's forearm stood out. With a makeshift needle with a rubber top like an eyedropper's, Jamie shot the drug into Freddie's arm.

What happened next shocked me. Freddie's eyes immediately closed and his mouth sagged open. I thought he was acting— nothing could make you high that fast. Jamie started laughing at Freddie, saying, "That shit is good, ain't it?" We could see Freddie fighting to get his eyes open. He looked at Jamie and tried to say yes, but all he could manage was a weak smile as he closed his eyes and his head began to tilt backward into the nod of oblivion the heroin had produced.

Jamie laughed again as he took the belt from around Freddie's arm and tied it around his own. He used his teeth to hold the end, pulling it tight so his own veins stood out while he injected himself with his other hand. He began to nod before he could get the needle out of his arm. We watched them both, not knowing what to do. Jamie had his eyes closed, his hand still on the needle in his arm.

"Wake him up," Tommy said to me.

"Naw, man. You wake him up. I don't know what he might do. That shit might make him crazy," I answered.

Before we could do anything, Jamie came out of his nod, looked around, half smiled at us looking at him, and removed the needle. He began to clean up as if nothing had happened. But every now and then, right in the middle of washing out the needle or putting his belt back on, he would be snatched away by the drug. His eyes would close, his knees would bend, drool would hang from his mouth, and then, just as we were convinced that he would crash to the floor, he would come out of it, stand up straight, and continue what he was doing as if he had never stopped.

After about fifteen minutes, Jamie and Freddie left for their Friday night on the town. Tommy and I sat there laughing and imitating how the older boys would suddenly nod out in the midst of talking or doing something. But even as I laughed, I wondered how they could use a drug that rendered them completely helpless for even a short time in the South Bronx. By the time I was a teenager my experience had shown me that the South Bronx was an extremely dangerous place. Any drug that inhibited my ability to defend myself was a drug I wanted nothing to do with. For fifteen minutes Jamie and Freddie, two guys with a reputation for being tough, were completely at the mercy of whoever happened to be in the room with them. That seemed like too much of a risk for me. So for me heroin was out.

Marijuana was a different story. In 1967 marijuana was still a fairly exotic drug on Union Avenue. All of the boys knew about it, but its price, five dollars for a "nickel bag," put it out of reach for guys who had to split the cost to buy a fifty-cent bottle of wine. The way the drug was used was dictated by its price. Typically, five to seven guys would chip in for a five-dollar bag of marijuana. The boy most expert in the art of rolling joints would roll up the entire bag. From one five-dollar bag you expected between fifteen and twenty joints. A nickel bag in 1967 was not a lot of marijuana, so you have to imagine how little pot was in each joint—not really much more than a dusting. After the joints were rolled, one of them was smoked by all the boys together and the rest were divided according to how much money each had contributed. Joints were considered too expensive to smoke a whole one by yourself, so most of the boys smoked with several other friends, all enjoying the comraderie of "getting high."

The first time I used marijuana, I was heading with Dennis, my best friend at the time, to Simpson Avenue, to the apartment of a girl we knew who was throwing a party. We were in the ninth grade in junior high school. We were sharing a pint of Thunderbird, too much for just the two of us, but we figured we would pass it around to the other boys from Union Avenue who'd be at the party. Dennis had sprung for the wine, since I only had the quarter it would cost me to get into the party. He and I were "boys." We had developed the close intimacy that boys of fifteen or sixteen feel for their best friends. That evening we were talking about our usual pre-party preoccupation, girls.

"Man, I'm gonna find me a honey and grind all night. Yo, check this out. This T-bird is better'n a motherfucker," Dennis said as he gulped some of the cold wine.

"You think *you* gonna grind. Man, watch out for me, cool breeze. I'm gonna break some poor girl's back." I wiped off the bottle neck with my hand, preparing to drink.

"You ever put a girl up against the wall and grind with her like that?"

"Naw, man. You?" I said, taking a swig. "Aw shit, man. This fucking shit taste like piss."

"Yeah. Last week over Sharon's house, she had that quarter party, did you go?"

"Naw. I didn't have any money."

"I was looking for you, man. You should have asked me. I would have let you cop a quarter to get into the gig. You my main man. You know you can always get a quarter from me. Here take this, man, but be cool. We don't want to be too fucked up once we get to the gig."

"I know. I was looking for you but you wasn't on the block. I looked in the cut and everywhere. I know you would have let me cop a quarter—we tight." I took another drink.

I slapped Dennis five and we continued to walk down the bitterly cold Bronx streets, leaning into the wind, our short leather jackets providing little warmth on this December night.

"Hey, Geoff. Guess what?"

"What?"

"I got a joint, man. Can you believe it? I got a joint. And I was saving it since Wednesday just for me and you. Nobody else. Can you dig it? Slap me five, man."

And for the second time I slapped Dennis five.

"You ever smoked a joint before?"

"Naw, man."

"It's easy. I did last week. It was cool. Nothing to it. You'll like it. You gonna get high with me?"

"Of course, man. You my main man."

Just like that I had made the decision. I'd never intended to use marijuana. Had thought about it from time to time but knew it wasn't for me. But Dennis was my best friend and I trusted him. If anybody messed with Dennis they had to mess with Geoff. If Dennis got a pair of Playboy shoes, I had to get a pair. Whenever anybody saw one of us, they asked where the other one was. I was shocked that he had used marijuana. But here he was going to the party with me, looking fine. And the buzz I had from the alcohol had made smoking a joint with my best friend seem like no big deal.

I asked, "How do you do it?"

"Watch me," Dennis said, as he turned his back to the wind, pulled out a book of matches, and lit the joint.

"You hold it like this, not like a cigarette," he said, putting the joint between his thumb and index finger. "Then you put it in your mouth and inhale like this."

Smoking one of our skinny joints was an art form in itself. They were so thin that it was very difficult to get air to pass through them. You couldn't pull on one of our joints the way you did with a cigarette because your cheeks would end up collapsing inward and you would end up inhaling very little smoke. Instead we put the joint, held between the tips of the thumb and first finger, up to our lips, and, allowing a small amount of air to pass around our fingers, we sucked at it.

"Once you inhale the smoke, you suck in some air like this," Dennis said while puckering his lips and sucking at the air like he had an imaginary straw in his mouth. "Then you hold your breath for as long as possible. You dig?" Dennis said this last line while trying to keep holding his breath.

"Yeah, man. I dig. Let me try." I reached for the joint. I pulled on it but it took several tries before I saw the end of the joint glow, indicating that I had actually smoked some of it. I imitated Dennis sucking in air, holding my breath, waiting to see what smoking reefer really felt like.

"Aw, man, you wet the motherfucker up. Don't slob on it. Keep your lips on your fingers, not on the joint. I don't want to be smoking no joint with your spit all over it. Here, watch me." Dennis repeated the procedure again.

In no time I got the hang of it. We smoked the joint, pulling on it, sipping on air, and holding our breath. And I waited to see what the high felt like. Dennis put the joint out after we had smoked half of it. He said we would smoke the rest on the way home.

"Are you high, man? Wasn't that shit good?"

"Yeah, man. It was better'n a motherfucker," I lied. The truth was I thought I felt high for a little while but I didn't know if it was from the joint or just dizziness from holding my breath. I decided that the most impressive thing about getting high was the technique of inhaling, keeping your lips off the joint, and holding your breath. What I didn't know was that there was so little marijuana in the joints we smoked that almost all of the high we got was due to a placebo effect. Most of what we were smoking was the rolling paper. It would be some years later, when my friends and I had more money, that I would discover how potent a drug marijuana is.

My friends and I were not the only ones discovering drugs in the sixties. It seemed that my entire generation was turning on. We got zooted, and bombed, wrecked, fucked up, and things were far out. We tripped and had speed raps that lasted all night. And somehow, after all was said and done, we managed to have enough functioning brain cells to get jobs or attend college. And many of us laughed at those crazy years of using drugs and indulging in excesses of every kind. As the years went by, many of us had enough bad experiences with drugs to give them up. So today when we hear about kids smoking pot and drinking, many of us remember when we did the same things and we think their experience mirrors ours. But what we might not realize is that, as far as teens and drugs are concerned, this ain't the sixties.

Patterns of alcohol and marijuana use among children today, we have to understand, are dramatically different. The drugs of choice for many of them, marijuana and alcohol, are linked together and actually marketed *to* children, and to boys in particular. This linking is done by certain alcohol manufacturers who have sunk to a new low, contracting with rap stars who make records glorifying marijuana to sell their malt liquor. Turn on the television and tune to videos that appeal to inner-city youth, and there they are. So for children the rap star is not just selling malt liquor, he is selling the whole lifestyle of drug and alcohol use. These commercials are targeted to inner-city youth, but they reach a much wider audience. The names of the malt liquors that our children drink may be unfamiliar to you, but thanks to the alcohol manufacturers' tactics they are known to almost all young people: Schlitz Malt Liquor, Colt 45, Olde English 800, and St. Ides, to name just a few.

What's worse, popular rap stars and other entertainers suggest a use pattern for these drugs that is excessive beyond excuse. Take malt liquor. Malt liquor has been around for a long time. When I was growing up, the brand Colt 45 was popular with some teens.

Malt liquor tends to contain more alcohol than plain beer (as high as 8 percent for some malt liquors, as compared to about 4 percent for beer). The big difference is that today malt liquor is sold in forty-ounce bottles, and these "forties" are now considered a single serving. When I was growing up, several boys would share a quart of beer or malt liquor; it's not uncommon today to see a group of boys all of whom have their own forties of malt liquor.

A fourteen- or fifteen-year-old boy weighing not more than a hundred and twenty pounds guzzling forty ounces of malt liquor is bad enough. But young people today are combining their drinking with smoking marijuana, not the skinny marijuana joints that some of us smoked while growing up, but "blunts." A blunt is made by taking the tobacco out of a cigar and replacing it with marijuana. The tobacco wrapping from a cigar burns slower than cigarette paper, so you not only have a larger marijuana cigarette, you have one that burns very slowly, so it doesn't burn up the marijuana when it's lit but not actually being smoked. Today many teens are growing up in a world where a forty and a blunt are part of a good time.

When I talk to teens about drinking forties and smoking blunts they tell me, "It's just beer and herb—no big deal." But the consumption patterns are so excessive that even with these "soft" drugs, young people's minds are being completely twisted when they indulge.

There is another problem with the way young people are using drugs today. When young people are bombed out of their minds, judgment is impaired to the extent that they will try things they would never have considered otherwise. I am particularly worried about the increasing use of heroin among young people. My generation knew that heroin was a terrible drug, and those of us growing up in the South Bronx knew it firsthand, from what we saw in the streets. But children today have grown up thinking that crack is the terrible drug. They know little about heroin. Because it takes longer to become addicted to heroin than to crack, many young people are being fooled into thinking that heroin is a fairly benign drug. And pushers are now selling heroin that is very pure and very cheap. The purity of this drug today means that users become just as addicted by snorting it or smoking it as they used to do by injecting it. So those who are beginning to use heroin in these ways, thinking they are safer than if they were shooting up, are dead wrong. We need to get a clear message out to our children now about the dangers of this drug.

So what should we tell boys about drugs? We should give them useful information, not our own biases. We should tell them the facts, which means we should become informed ourselves. Boys will reject out of hand sweeping generalities about drugs, such as that all drugs are equally dangerous. We should learn not only about drugs that might have been around when we were teens— like marijuana, amphetamines, and heroin—but also about the new drugs teens are using, like the "designer drug" Ecstasy and Special K (ketamine, an animal tranquilizer). We should make sure to enlist the support of other young people, those closer in age to teens, to talk to them about the dangers of drugs. The reason so many of my closest friends escaped the heroin epidemic of the sixties was that one teenager we looked up to, Mike, went out of his way to point out the living truth of addiction. We need to find young people willing to be spokespersons to other young people about the dangers of drugs. In some communities teen chapters of Narcotics Anonymous or Alcoholics Anonymous might fulfill this need.

After giving boys the facts, I recommend that you tell them how you feel, why you think using drugs is dangerous. And what should you say if your son asks you if you ever used drugs? There is no one answer for this question. It involves many factors that parents will have to weigh for themselves. But in general I think we have to be honest. If we did use drugs we should tell our children about it. I have found in talking to teens that they really appreciate someone who is willing to talk honestly with them about drugs. Teens are like the rest of us, they tend to find information more credible if it comes from someone who has actually had experience in the area they are talking about.

Boys need to know where we stand on drug use—we have to make it clear and unambiguous that we are against it. This does not mean we don't recognize that most boys will experiment with drugs and alcohol, it means that we give them a consistent message that we think drugs are dangerous for their bodies and their minds. Dealers never tell boys that drugs are bad, and most of their peers won't either. And no matter who else we count on to educate our boys about the dangers of drugs, it is our own voices that count the most. When it comes to drugs, this is not the time to be timid or equivocate. We must make sure our position is so solid that no matter what new tremors or upheavals happen in our boys' lives, they will know where we stand.

Faith

THE YOUNG MAN sitting in my office was atypical in that he came to us with so much going for him. Scott was a fairly new member of Rheedlen's student workforce. He'd started by doing what most new students do, maintenance work. I knew he was going to a prep school and was a good student. It was Brian who pointed out to me that Scott had been in a fight and that I needed to talk with him. I called Scott into my office. From the nervousness he displayed I decided that the first thing to do was put him somewhat at ease. Having spent no real time with Scott, I studied him for a moment. I saw before me a powerfully built young man of dark complexion, with bright inquisitive eyes. I could tell immediately that he had been brought up to have good manners and to be respectful of adults.

"I heard you had a fight. Well, from the looks of things you didn't do so bad. I don't see any bruises," I began. His smile reflected his realization that this wasn't going to be a lecture on fighting, but it faded almost as quickly as it had appeared as he raised his hand and showed me a bandage.

"I got cut," he said.

I had been concerned that Scott would resist my wanting to talk with him. One look in his eyes showed me that he wanted—needed—to talk to someone.

"The guy tried to kill me. At least I think he was trying to kill me. You know . . . sometimes it's hard to tell." I could tell he had been thinking about this for a long time. Turning it over and over in his head.

"Why don't you tell me what happened," I said.

"Well, last week I was hanging out with one of my friends on the train. He wasn't a good friend, but I knew him from around my block. I go to parochial school but I still hang out with guys from on the block. You know? I mean, I don't think I'm better than anyone else, or I won't hang with you if you go to public school."

Scott was in the predicament that many young men find themselves in if they are academic achievers and live in inner-city neighborhoods. Other boys are always testing you to see if you think you are better than they are. If they believe that you think so, then watch out: you become a target and might be jumped, robbed, threatened, humiliated, or ostracized. So if you're a boy like Scott, you walk a thin line. You try to be friendly and hang out with boys that provide you with social cover; the more friends you have who are known as tough kids on the block, the better your chances of not being targeted for abuse.

"While we were on the train we met this kid my friend knew. He didn't know him that well, but he said he was all right. The kid said he had just gotten out of jail. He invited us to hang out with him on his block. Later that night I went over there with my friend to meet this kid, and another kid tried to take my new goose-down coat. I don't know if it was a setup or what. One minute we're talking on the stoop with this kid we just met, the next minute this other kid comes up and demands my coat."

"What did you do?" I asked.

"I told him no way. Then he started calling me names and saying how he was going to take my coat and all this stuff. I told him, 'If you want to fight, let's fight.' I mean, the kid wasn't all that big. He was kind of skinny. I wasn't afraid of him. So we started fighting."

"What did the other two kids do? You know, the kid you came with and the other kid you met on the train. What did they do?"

"They didn't do nothing. They didn't even leave the stoop. I mean, it was kind of strange. I was fighting this kid on the sidewalk and I think they just kept on talking. That's why I don't know if it was a setup or what."

"Okay, so you're fighting with this kid. How did you get cut?" I asked.

"That's the strange part. The kid had the knife in his hand all the time. You know, it was dark and I was kind of—you know—not scared, but like not completely aware. So this kid is punching me but I have on this thick goose-down coat so I don't really feel nothing. Then he swings for my neck and I block it, but the knife cuts me on the back of my neck. Then I really look at the kid and I see the knife. I also see feathers floating down toward the ground and I realize he wasn't punching me, he was trying to stab me. But my coat is real thick and he couldn't stab me through all those feathers. But my coat is all cut up and feathers are coming out of it. So he swings for my neck again and I grab his hand and try to take the knife away. And my hand gets cut by the knife while I'm trying to wrestle it away. Then he gets the knife away from me."

"And what were the others doing while this guy was trying to cut you with the knife?"

"They still didn't do nothing."

"So what did you do?"

"I ran. I mean, when he pulled the knife away I pushed him and he was off balance. Then I jetted. I ran home."

I knew I had to address what Scott must have been grappling with all weekend. "The guy was trying to kill you, wasn't he?"

"Yeah. He was trying to kill me. Over a coat. I mean he was going to kill me over a *coat*. And the stupid thing is, he was trying to stab me in the side and I would have bled all over the coat so he wouldn't have been able to wear it."

"And you didn't even know the guy was trying to kill you?"

"No. No, that's what's so weird. We was fighting. I thought he was punching me and I was thinking to myself how if I really tried to hurt this guy maybe his friend would jump in. So I wasn't even trying to hurt him. And he was trying to kill me. If it wasn't for how thick my coat was, I would be dead."

I could tell by the look in his eye that he was pondering what so many people who look death in the eye and survive think about—why did I survive when by all rights I should be dead? I asked him a question that I have found myself asking more and more children who come to me in crisis. It's funny, I've worked with children for over twenty years and just within the last couple of years I've begun to ask what might be one of the most important questions to put to young people in these situations.

"Do you believe in God?"

The question drew that funny look most young people give me when I ask them about their belief in God. Scott was no different. The look that came over his face was one of pure surprise.

"Yes, I do," he answered.

"Good. I know you're trying to figure out why you weren't hurt worse. Or killed by that kid. Whenever you face a life-or-death situation your mind gets forced to deal with the larger picture." I explained to Scott that I've known too many kids who escape death only to become convinced that there is no order to life, that life is a series of random events and you could die at any time. They actually begin to act more recklessly, believing that they could die at any moment so there's no reason to take precautions. But some of us who believe in God—or Muhammad, or Jehovah, or Buddha—can use events like the one Scott survived to re-affirm our faith. We become more convinced that God does exist and that our escape from death was more proof of that. "Is any of this making sense to you?" I asked.

Scott nodded his head yes, but he still seemed stunned by the turn of the conversation.

"Now let me tell you something. Your life being spared was not just dumb luck. God has a special plan for you. You have to figure out what it is and do the right thing. And by the way, whatever the plan is, it's *not* for you to hang out with ex-convicts you don't know." Scott's smile and warm handshake as he left my office convinced me that he was pleased that I had broached the subject of faith with him. We are sure he will go on to college and do important things with his life, never forgetting his brush with death on a dark Harlem street but being stronger for surviving it.

Having been trained as a professional to keep a clear separation between church and state, I never used to ask children about their religious upbringing. I never questioned that faith was an individual issue to be acted on by families, not outsiders. But something happened to change my way of thinking about children and faith.

I was holding a session with teenagers on violence and posed the question, "When is it right to kill?"

One young boy's answer shocked me. "When somebody is going to kill you. I mean, you just can't kill somebody because they look at you wrong, or they dis you. But if they gonna kill me, I'm gonna kill them."

"You mean you think it's all right to kill somebody if they're after you?" I asked.

"I mean, it's not all right. I mean—check it out—it's not like it was back in the day when you was a kid. I mean, on the real deal a man gotta do what a man gotta do. You know what I mean? I mean if you know someone is after you and they got a gun, what're you gonna do? Stay upstairs forever? Never come outside? Or just get killed? Get real, man. You gonna get your gun and get him first."

The nodding heads of the other boys confirmed that they too believed what they'd just heard. I kept wondering whatever happened to Thou Shall Not Kill. I knew I shouldn't ask, but I had to.

"What about God?'

"What do you mean, God?"

"God. You know. God. Don't you believe in God?"

The boy looked at the others, his face asking them if I was for real. Then he answered.

"Okay. You really want to know what I think? All right, you serious so I'll be serious. If there was a God would he let things be like this? Look at this shit, man. People killing one another, kids selling drugs, mothers leaving their babies to get high. Look how people living—like roaches. Garbage everywhere. And why God pick on us? I didn't do anything to God. Why he make my life so miserable? Naw, man, ain't no God. Any God would let people without nothing always get fucked over, while those with money don't give a fuck, ain't my kind of God. If there is a God he's on the side of rich people. Rich people invented that God thing so they can keep fucking over the poor and poor people won't fight for a piece of the pie. That's what I think."

Again the heads of the other boys were nodding, and I could tell that the one spoke for the many. I looked at these young men and realized that they were all struggling to survive in a cultural context that did not include religion. And if religion did not act as a mitigating force on the constant assault of contemporary culture, with its empty values and excessive violence, what had become the guiding principle of life for these young men? For many of them the answer was consumption. They measured their lives and self-worth by how many pairs of sneakers they had, how many pairs of jeans, how many designer jackets. And—like so much of America—they were obsessed with money. You got it any way you could get it. The end justified the means.

So what forces exist to counter the commercial bombardment and the prevailing pressure on boys to fulfill the stereotypes of being male—conquerors of women, violent, non-sensitive— that they encounter every day? Where are boys supposed to get their values? This becomes particularly important when we consider how corrupt the world looks to many children growing up today. Just think about it. Everyone looks as if he or she is sneaking, lying, cheating, and doing anything possible to get money. The president of the United States has a sexual harassment suit pending and the Whitewater scandal hanging over his head, and seemingly a new scandal in his administration every week. The Speaker of the House has been fined three hundred thousand dollars for his own political misdeeds. The Rodney King beating demonstrated that police sometimes act like common criminals. Children see and hear about scandals all the time. For many boys, when there is no church or other religious community, when there is no strong extended family, the only place to sort out right from wrong is on the streets. I recognize that church alone is not enough to support the development of a strong moral base, that we must have strong families and strong communities as well. But it is one of the few societal structures that has as its mission the teaching of moral values. For me, it took the church and then some to straighten me out.

My faith life was colored by the fact that my maternal grandfather and grandmother were both ordained Baptist ministers.

During my youth I watched as my grandfather moved up the church hierarchy until he became the pastor of Mount Pleasant Baptist Church, located in Harlem. Even when I was a young boy, my grandparents, with their straightforward honesty and morality, seemed out of sync with the rest of the world that surrounded us in the South Bronx. I kept one eye on them and one eye trained warily on the other world, not convinced that good would finally triumph over evil. The God my grandparents worshiped was a demanding God. For them God brokered no compromises. Neither did they. They demanded absolute honesty, absolute morality, absolute chastity.

Mount Pleasant Baptist Church was located on 137th Street, and was one of the many small churches that are scattered all over Harlem in brownstones or small buildings. The people of Mount Pleasant were friendly, and church started and ended with handshaking and smiles, but the service itself was serious business. The pastors, Reverend Brown, and later my grandfather, Reverend Williams, were fire-and-brimstone preachers. Church service for me suggested mysteries and dangers I could only imagine.

We sat amazed and often bewildered as we heard about heaven and hell, devils and angels, lost souls and the power of the Holy Ghost. Gospel music was blended into the service so that a momentum was gradually built that reached a crescendo that had the parishioners "shouting" in the aisles and fainting in the choir stand. This was the most frightening part of the service for me because I lived in terror that the Holy Spirit would take over my grandmother or my mother and they would be the ones shouting next to me. So there I was on many a Sunday when the service was at its peak and my grandmother would begin waving her hand, shouting and praying "Thank you Jesus." I for my part would be praying for God to skip over Grandma and not let her get the Holy Ghost. The more excited Grandma got, the harder I prayed for God to calm her down.

My first crisis of faith came before I entered elementary school and was caused by a boy my age named Warren. Warren lived next door to us and by our definition was a bad boy. Warren would tell lies, sneak into the street, and talk bad about adults. My brothers and I were all quite shocked by his behavior. One day I had had enough. I knew enough about religion at five that I figured I had to turn Warren from his evil ways.

"Warren, you shouldn't tell stories because if you do you won't go to heaven."

"There ain't no such thing as heaven."

"Yes there is. You better not say things like that because God will hear you and get you."

"There ain't no God."

With that declaration we all stared at Warren with eyes wide. How could he say such a thing?

"You better take that back, Warren. God's gonna send you to hell with the Devil and you gonna burn in fire."

"No, I ain't gonna go to no hell. You see I'm still here. If there was a God he would've sent me to hell."

"Well, if you keep it up he gonna kill you with a lightning bolt. You gonna get kilt, I'm warning you."

"Well, let him try to kill me. C'mon, God, kill me," Warren yelled to the heavens. "See—nothing happened. Ain't nothing gonna happen."

"God didn't kill you cause you didn't do a big enough sin. I know what God will kill you for."

"What?"

My brother Dan was looking at me now with that look in his eye. He knew I was intentionally baiting Warren to get him to do something to get him killed by God. But before he could intervene I set the trap.

"If you say a curse word God will kill you with a lightning bolt."

"No he won't," Warren replied.

"Oh yes he will," Dan answered, not willing to have Warren's death on his conscience.

"I'm gonna say a curse," Warren said.

"You better not. I'm warning you. God is gonna get you," I said, hoping Warren didn't heed my warning and actually said a curse. I wondered how this whole lightning bolt thing worked. Did you just disappear? Was there maybe only a small pile of brown dust left afterwards? It wasn't that I wanted Warren to die—he was all right. But if he wanted to mess with God, well, there was nothing I could do. And besides, it would be fun to talk about it at dinner that night.

"I'm gonna say one right now. Watch!" We all drew away from Warren, squinting our eyes, waiting for the lightning.

"Shit!" We waited. "Fuck!" Our mouths fell open and we took another step backwards away from him.

"Shit, shit, shit. Fuck, fuck, fuck. There. You see? Nothing."

We stared at Warren in amazement. There he was, smiling and cursing and nothing happened to him. Why not? The adults had told us that God would kill you on the spot for sinning. Did they lie to us? But lying was a sin. Did they commit a sin? I watched Warren for the next few weeks, thinking maybe God was just too busy to get to him right then. But Warren survived and my faith in God was shaken.

I never told my mother or grandparents about Warren, but I questioned them constantly about God and religion. And I began to experiment with religion to see if what I was told was true. I would go to a place where I was alone and I would say a curse under my breath to see what God would do. And when God did nothing about my cursing, I decided I would tell small lies to see if God would punish me or reveal the truth to my mother. And when I realized that no one seemed to be able to tell if I was telling the truth or lying, I became more certain that while I believed there was a God, he was not paying nearly as close attention as my grandparents thought.

Because we went to church every Sunday, once a week I was confronted with my beliefs on God. I was full of childish questions and my grandmother did her best to answer them. Many years later I realized that those question-and-answer periods were part of my formative cognitive development. There are no questions more mind expanding than those that deal with life and death, good and evil. My grandmother had the patience of a saint and I the slyness of a fox as I tried with my best five-year-old intellect to discover what God was.

"Grandma, how do you know there is a God?"

"I know. I have faith."

"But how do you really know? Have you ever seen him?"

"No person can see God. We are taught to have faith. Do you know what faith is?"

"No."

"Faith is when you believe something even when you can't prove it's true. A person with faith can do anything."

"Can a person with faith jump off a building and live?"

"Yes, if their faith is strong enough."

"Can a person jump off the Empire State Building and live?"

"Yes . . . well . . . I mean, a person wouldn't do that. But if God wanted a person to do that, that person would be able to do it."

"Is God the strongest person in the world?"

"God is stronger than any person or any thing. He is smarter than any person and knows everything there is, everything there was, and everything there will ever be."

"If God knows everything and can do anything, what does he want from us?"

"He wants us to be good and obey his commandments."

"Why doesn't he just make us good? He knows who the good

people are and who the evil people are. Why doesn't he just make the evil people good?"

"God has his reasons. Often God tests us like Job. Let me tell you the story. In the Bible there is a story about a man named Job . . ."

I was fascinated when Grandma told me of things that happened in the Bible. But from the story of Job I could only grasp that God was not fair. Why would he make a person suffer so badly? Why, if God was so powerful, couldn't he have taught the same lesson more mercifully? This question of the fairness of God began to haunt me as I got older. People were not honest, did not treat one another with Christian love and respect. The world was a dog-eat-dog place where the strong took advantage of the weak. I was a small boy during the civil rights struggle, and the television and newspapers bombarded us with Bible-toting white Southerners who hung black men from trees and called them niggers; while some black ministers preached nonviolence, we lived in a violent world, and for many of us the concept of nonviolence seemed suicidal. And more radical groups began to shout that religion was the opium of the people. When I would go into Mount Pleasant Baptist Church as a teenager it seemed ludicrous to me that my grandfather would be in the pulpit preaching about personal sin to the same people every Sunday while all around him Harlem seemed to be falling apart. How could he be spending so much time saving the saved when the people who needed saving were on the streets on Sunday and not in church?

Over the years my disenchantment grew with a religion that I felt was out of touch. By the time I was fifteen I had rejected the church as irrelevant. I now joined the boys that I used to pass on my way to church, who played football on Sunday. And like other boys all over the country we developed our own set of values and norms. And we laughed at those people who strolled to church on Sundays and we thought they were the misguided ones and we were the enlightened. And when those adults around us defined us as bad boys we didn't try to defend ourselves. In fact, we embraced their definition of us and strutted our "badness" in broad daylight for all to see.

I see my attitude as a teenager reflected in the behavior and values of many boys today. They are lost in a wilderness of half-truths and throwaway values that are embraced one day, when it is convenient, and discarded the next when they get in the way of what they want. Boys are being taught early that the only thing that is important is to achieve success and that you can do so by any means you can get away with, even as they are being preached at to be moral and to play by the rules. And when adults focus on boys, it's typically on the outside—how they look, what their grades are, and how well they play sports—not on the inside. No one is gauging whether an internal moral compass is pointing them in a direction that leads to morality, honesty, and enlightenment. Indeed, when you talk to boys about what they feel about themselves and about the world, you often hear statements that are nihilistic. Many see the world as comprised of a series of obstacles to overcome and opportunities to exploit; they see no sense of universal truths. And many of them have no faith.

It may be an oversimplification to say these young men have no faith. Many have faith in things: cars, computers, guns for some. But they don't have faith that things will turn out all right. The kind of faith that leads to hope even when there seems to be no empirical evidence to support being hopeful. This kind of faith is essential for all of us, and many boys lose it very early in life. To me there is nothing more frightening than to look into the eyes of a nine-year-old and see no sign of hope, to see that at that tender age they have given up. I have heard even younger children who when being asked about some wrongful deed say, "Do what you want to me. I don't care." And they mean it. They don't care. For them life has already become so hard, so hopeless, that they know nothing you could say or do to them could even come close to touching the sense of despair they feel inside.

We must remember that children often go through experiences that might seem minor or trivial to us but are traumatic for them. They fail subjects in school, their boyfriend or girlfriend leaves them, someone says they are ugly, or fat, or stupid. And boys are in a particular quandary because they are taught not to talk about their feelings, and often not to show them. Adults sometimes make it harder for boys to come to us by saying things like "What's the big deal?" or "Don't worry, you'll get over it." For many boys it *is* a big deal, and many don't get over it. You can look at the suicide rates for boys in this country and know that too many boys think that there is nothing for them to live for. Boys start off with the same suicide rates as girls, but starting at about age nine the rate for boys begins a steady and troubling climb. From age ten to fourteen, the boys' rate is double that of girls. From fifteen to nineteen the boys' rate is four times higher. Between the ages of twenty to twenty-four the suicide rate for young men is six times higher than the rate for young women (U.S. Bureau of Health and Human Services, National Center for Health Statistics, *Vital Statistics of the United States*, 1991, vol. 2, part A, p. 51).

These numbers indicate only successful suicides. There are hundreds of thousands of boys who have attempted suicide but did not die, and there are many more who could be classified as suicidal just by their lifestyle of excessive drugs, violence, and unprotected sex.

Boys who are not connected with a formal faith institution like a church, synagogue, or mosque often miss out on another important concept these institutions bring into our lives—the concept of forgiveness. Boys need to be forgiven when they have done things that they know are wrong. Someone who matters has to say, "I know you did a bad thing, but you are not a bad person." We have to realize that some boys do bad things over and over. And this is one reason that there must be other adults besides parents in boys' lives who can forgive them. I have had plenty of parents come into my office, fed up with a boy, saying, "He's never going to change. I give up." And when you look at what that boy has done and how many times he has done it, you can understand why a parent could think that there was no hope for turning his life around. Children are most at risk when parents themselves have given up hope. We therefore have to make sure that there are always other people in a boy's life who haven't given up on him— a family member, a teacher, or a mentor. I know from experience that if adults hang in there, boys often do change. This doesn't mean that we suddenly become pushovers, that we allow boys to escape unpunished or undisciplined after wrongful acts. It does mean that we always give them the message of salvation and forgiveness with our chastisements. It is important that even when we are at our wits' end we don't say things like "There's no hope for you" or "I can tell you'll never change." We need to say—and this is what many faith leaders are good at saying to young people—"I know you can change."

Boys also need to be taught how to forgive themselves. I have seen boys do one or two bad things and internalize the reaction of parents—or teachers, or the police, or peers—to the extent that they really believe they are "bad" or "no good" or "heading for trouble." Boys who get in trouble often have no mechanism in their lives to wipe the slate clean, to get back to neutral again— no way of reconciling what they did with who they are. And there are many influences, both real-life (drug dealers and gangbangers) and artistic (rap music, videos, movies), that reinforce and even expand on their sense of themselves as bad. We have to ensure that even as we forgive boys, we work with them to help them forgive themselves, to redefine themselves as honest, trustworthy, and decent.

Boys need to be grounded in faith. They need real and honest discussions about right and wrong, good and evil. These conversations must not end when they are young children, but must be constantly revisited. As boys begin puberty and the world becomes more complex, less black-and-white, they need more from us that helps them develop their values and their faith. Some of what we must do has to be direct—talking with them about their beliefs and ours regarding God, life after death, heaven and hell. Some has to be more subtle—exposing them to great works of art, music, and poetry that have faith as an underlying theme. We can make sure our boys read and learn about the real-life struggles of men and women whose overcoming of hardship is the definition of faith. We can have them read about Martin Luther King, Jr., Mahatma Gandhi, Joan of Arc—such stories can be found in the histories of every race, religion, and ethnic group. In other words, we must do not one thing but many things when boys are young and as they get older to ensure that they have a solid foundation of faith in their lives before they ever need it.

In 1972, probably the most difficult year of my life, I learned a tough lesson about faith. I was in Maine, at Bowdoin College, and it was my sophomore year. I had twin sons born that year, and I was devastated when one of them died of Sudden Infant Death Syndrome. My brother John, who was one year older than I, died in Texas that same year. And when I found out soon afterward that my grandmother was dying from cancer, I simply lost faith.

I might have been able to accept one of these deaths, but not all three. Why had God taken my infant son, my brother whom I worshiped, and now my grandmother whom I cherished? The answer to me was that there simply was no God. Not only did I doubt the existence of God, but my own life lost meaning. Why was I working so hard in college, away from my family and friends, sacrificing so much, when death could come at any instant, making all of my hard work folly?

When I went home to see my grandmother she was bedridden. The cancer had robbed her of her strength and would soon take her life. Right before I went back to school I went into her room and I asked her the question that was tearing me apart. I know it was selfish of me to ask her this while she lay dying, but I had to know.

"Grandma, do you still believe in God?'

"Of course I do. Why do you ask me that?"

"Because you're sick. You have cancer."

"Being sick doesn't have anything to do with faith."

"But how can you have faith when God has done this to you? Made you suffer. And for what? What did you do to offend God so much that you have to be in pain like this?"

"Geoffrey, listen to me. I know you've been through so much with the loss of your son, and your brother. But don't lose faith in God or yourself. God has a plan and you're part of it, so you can't give up. Faith is not something you believe in until things don't go your way. It's not like rooting for a football team and then when they start losing changing sides and rooting for another team. Faith means you believe no matter what.

"Do you hear me? It's easy to have faith when you have a million dollars and you're in perfect health. Do you think that proves anything to God? Your problem is that you think if you study your books hard enough you will find all the answers. All the answers aren't in books. They never will be. So do I still believe in God? Yes. More now than ever before."

I reluctantly went back to Bowdoin after spending a week with my grandmother, not knowing that this was to be the last time I would ever talk with or see her. She died within weeks of my leaving. I spent the rest of my sophomore year in a daze, the combined losses too much for me to comprehend. But I knew I had to keep trying, not lose my faith, because that's what my grandmother wanted. And when I became suddenly frightened, or depressed, and found that my faith was weak and couldn't sustain me, I felt that I could borrow some of my grandmother's faith. Even though she was no longer alive, her faith was real and tangible to me. Many a night I leaned on her faith when I felt my own couldn't support my doubts.

Every child needs a grandmother like mine in their lives—a person who is older, and wiser, and is willing to fight for as long as it takes for that child's soul. A person who is willing to hold his or her own life up as an example of faith. A person who both forgives and teaches forgiveness. A person whose abundance of faith will be there in sufficient supply when children need it. Because sooner or later children need more faith than they possess. That's where we come in.

Work

IT WAS REPORT CARD day and the young people knew that their grades at school would have a direct bearing on whether or not they could continue to work at Rheedlen. We had become used to the necessity for vigilance on our part on report card day after one particularly creative incident. At first Brian, who is my assistant at Rheedlen, was delighted when he made the announcement in my office. He was talking about a group of young people who work for us.

"Geoff, we finally did it."

"Did what?" I asked.

"We got them all to pass all of their classes this marking period. The turnaround is remarkable. Two of them went from failing one class and barely passing the others, to good grades in all their classes. Can you believe it?"

"Are you sure?" I asked.

"I checked all of the report cards myself. It's the first time everyone has passed everything."

"Well, that's great," I said. "Let's make sure we let them know how proud we are of them."

We weren't proud for long. Brian's eye for detail found a coincidence too odd to be accepted at face value. It seemed that on three of the boys' report cards a zero had printed slightly off line. When he compared their report cards with those of other high school students who worked for us and went to the same school, he found that their zeros were printed correctly. It was an almost perfect job. The boys had created the computerized report cards using the skills that they had learned at Rheedlen and had changed failing grades to passing ones. A call to the high school confirmed our suspicions; the boys had failed several classes. They were suspended but told that they could reapply for work at Rheedlen when they brought us real report cards with all passing grades. Next semester they got passing grades the old-fashioned way, by earning them. The three have passed all of their classes ever since and all have completed their requirements for graduation.

The academic turnaround these boys accomplished in the end is not unusual. Many of the young people who work for Rheedlen graduate from high school and go on to college because of one thing—work. We have found work to be a very effective tool in keeping boys involved in school. For millions of teenagers growing up in America, school is something that they feel only marginally connected to. To them schoolwork seems disconnected from their lives. They complain that it's boring and find it irrelevant. But they want to work. Tying the two together has pushed many a Rheedlen boy through high school and into college.

Learning how to work early on in life is important for all children, but it is critical for poor children, especially boys. Work provides a much-needed source of money to buy the necessities of life. It teaches children how to save and budget. It teaches real responsibility. Working as a child helps teach the values and ethics surrounding employment at an early age. And, finally, it connects poor boys to a world that is unknown to many of them, a world of working adults and the normative behaviors that are associated with working for a living. So work should be part of every poor child's life experience, but there is one huge problem: in many poor communities jobs and job opportunities have all but disappeared. And the group that finds it hardest to get a job is boys.

Sociologist and author William Julius Wilson, in his book *When Work Disappears* (1996), explains why in some communities, especially poor African-American communities, finding work has become all but impossible. "The disappearance of work in many inner-city neighborhoods is in part related to the nationwide decline in the fortunes of low-skilled workers. Fundamental structural changes in the new global economy, including changes in the distribution of jobs and in the level of education required to obtain employment, resulted in the simultaneous occurrence of increasing joblessness and declining real wages for low-skilled workers. The decline of the mass production system, the decreasing availability of lower-skilled blue-collar jobs, and the growing importance of training and education in the higher-growth industries adversely affected the employment rates and earnings of low-skilled black workers, many of whom are concentrated in inner-city ghettos. The growing suburbanization of jobs has aggravated the employment woes of poor inner-city workers. Most ghetto residents cannot afford an automobile and therefore have to rely on public transit systems that make the connection between inner-city neighborhoods and suburban job locations difficult and time-consuming" (p. 54).

And to make matters worse, many poor minority residents face a well-developed set of negative perceptions about their skills and abilities. This is particularly true for black males. Wilson cites the Urban Poverty and Family Life Study's survey of "a representative sample of Chicago-area employers," which indicates "that many consider inner-city workers—especially young black males—to be uneducated, unstable, uncooperative, and dishonest" (p. 111).

We have in our country a very large number of youth who are growing up in communities that have failing schools, high rates of crime, and a myriad other social problems. We must find real solutions for those problems, but we must also understand that the absence of the opportunity for work creates another set of problems many of us have not considered. Wilson writes, "Neighborhoods that offer few legitimate employment opportunities, inadequate job information networks, and poor schools lead to the disappearance of work. That is, where jobs are scarce, where people rarely, if ever, have the opportunity to help their friends and neighbors find jobs, and where there is a disruptive or degraded school life purporting to prepare youngsters for eventual participation in the work force, many people eventually lose their feeling of connectedness to work in the formal economy; they no longer expect work to be a regular, and regulating, force in their lives. In the case of young people, they may grow up in an environment that lacks the idea of work as a central experience of adult life—they have little or no labor-force attachment. These circumstances also increase the likelihood that the residents will rely on illegitimate sources of income, thereby further weakening their attachment to the legitimate labor market"(pp. 52–53).

It is paramount that we reconnect young people to the world of work. There are great models of how to do this effectively, like Youth Build, a national program that combines real on-the-job work experience with academic support for young people. There is also the Summer Youth Employment Program (SYEP), a government program designed to provide poor youth with opportunities for summer employment. Each year SYEP faces an uphill battle to keep its funding when we ought to be figuring out how to make the program a better one and expanding it to employ youth year-round.

But simply providing young people with jobs is not the solution to ensuring that young people learn how to work. At Rheedlen we find that we must train teenagers right from the beginning that a job carries with it a set of expectations that the young person might not understand or even agree with. There are the usual things that most employers expect from their employees—punctuality, good attendance, reliability. But then there are other things that we find we must instruct young people in—professional appearance, having a good attitude, respect for authority. Probably the most difficult thing our young people have to learn to cope with is how to do a good job even when you don't like doing something. It seems that many of them think they ought to like what they do for work all the time. If they don't, they often feel taken advantage of, or picked on by their supervisor, and many times they feel perfectly justified in making sure their supervisor is acutely aware of their unhappiness.

There was one time when we had several prominent members of President Clinton's cabinet coming to visit our Countee Cullen Beacon School. They were coming with David N. Dinkins, then mayor of New York. A host of news reporters were waiting and television cameras were everywhere. In the midst of making sure everything was prepared, we realized we needed someone to help set up the tables where a light snack would be served to the hundred or so dignitaries attending. I spotted two of our teen employees standing around and asked them to help carry the food and paper plates into the gymnasium where the event was being held.

"Excuse me, I want you two to help set up the snacks in the gym and then help serve our guests. Make sure you bring the paper plates and cups with you."

"We were told we were to do security," one answered.

"Well, that's okay because we have enough security. I need you to help with the food prep," I said.

"Nobody told us that we would be setting up and serving food. I'll be honest, I don't want to serve people food. That's not my job," said the other.

"Your job is to work for Rheedlen and do whatever we need you to do. Now I don't plan to have a big debate in the hallway. I have people who are grown men and women, who have degrees from college, helping with the food. You two help out like everybody else. That's the end of discussion," I replied.

As the president of Rheedlen I am not used to having employees balk at lending a helping hand to aid the company. Everyone at Rheedlen knows that I will roll up my sleeves as quick as the next person when something needs to be done. My directors all sweep floors, move tables, or set up food when the need arises. I have a reputation for being fair with employees, but I demand that they work hard and give us a good day's work for their pay. And when it comes to work I don't make exceptions for young people; they also must work hard. I assumed that after hearing the tone in my voice the two teenagers would put their reservations aside and do what was asked of them.

The complaints came rapidly one after another. It was not only adult staff who came to me, the other young people who worked for us noticed as well. These two particular boys had a terrible attitude and didn't care who knew it. I rushed into the gym. It was packed with some of the most influential people in New York City. People seemed excited about the visit and the question-and-answer session that was about to begin. Everyone seemed to be having a good time, everyone except two teenagers standing sullenly behind a table filled with juices, soft drinks, snacks, and paper products. When people asked for soda it was poured and handed to them with open hostility. I found two of my adult staff and quickly replaced the two teens.

The next day I brought the two into my office. I asked them why on such an important day they refused to be supportive. I reminded them that they knew Rheedlen well and knew we had high standards for all our employees. Why, I asked, when they were asked to do something, even if they didn't like it, had they responded in such an angry way? Their answer: they didn't know how other people felt about serving people, but they didn't like it. I realized that they thought they were too good to be serving people cups of juice. Now these were not teens who had money, or who came from homes that had money. They had no high school or college degrees, no professional training that would ensure that they could support themselves. Yet they were so proud that they felt serving juice was beneath them. They were unrepentant. They were fired.

The thing that struck me about this incident when it happened was that these two boys knew they were risking their jobs by their behavior. (After several months they came back to us with a new attitude toward work, and have been excellent employees ever since.) They felt they were standing up for some principle that had to do with their being exploited. They were proud that unlike the other teens, they had stood up for themselves. They were not the first teens that Rheedlen has fired because they refused to do hard work or did it with such anger that the children or adults that they were working with felt unwelcome.

I have talked with many young people who have gotten fired from their jobs, and when I've questioned why they were fired they say, "They didn't like me because I'm black," or Latino, or whatever. Or they say, "They were prejudiced there. They gave me all the dirty jobs and the other people had the easy jobs." Boys with no previous work experience seem to find it hardest to adjust to the world of employment. Boys often confuse their status as males with how they are treated on the job. They often feel disrespected and humiliated when a supervisor chastises them or orders them around. I'm not trying to suggest for a second that many teens don't face discrimination and racism, but they also fall victim to their own unrealistic expectations about work. They don't know that everybody starts at the bottom, that the lower the level of the skills that are needed to perform your job, the more likely you are to have to take orders, to be bossed, to do the dirty work.

I have found that many boys come to their first job with no real understanding of what hard work means. This is a tremendous handicap. Girls are often expected to take responsibility around the house, cooking, or cleaning, or doing the laundry. There is often a set of responsibilities and expectations placed on girls at home that helps prepare them for other work experiences. But much too often nothing of the sort is expected of boys. We know that much of being able to understand and excel in the workplace has to do with the attitudes, habits, and experiences we have had before we ever arrive at that first paying job. Many boys face real hard work for the first time when they get their first job—and they are totally unprepared for this new experience. And that is our fault. Parents and other adults don't begin early enough preparing children for the real world of work. When once children played an important part in the economy of many families, working in the fields or factories next to their parents, today many adults do everything possible to make sure their children don't have to do hard work. This, in my opinion, is a mistake. I learned how to work hard before I ever earned a penny for it. Again, it was a lesson learned from my grandmother.

My grandparents' house in Wyandanch was set on about three-quarters of an acre of land. When they moved in the house was completed, but the yard had to be landscaped by us. We had no money to hire a professional landscaper. The front yard was a mess. It had been graded only slightly after the workers finished the house, and grass and weeds sprouted willy-nilly. Grandma explained what we had to do to the yard before we could plant grass.

"First we have to pull up all the grass and weeds, then pick up all the big pieces of wood and rocks and stuff like that. Then when we finish that we have to rake the ground even and pick up the smaller pieces of debris that we find."

I couldn't wait to get started. The quicker we began, the quicker we could plant the grass, and then I would have my own lush lawn to play on. Grandma gave me a pair of work gloves and I felt like a real grownup. I attacked the yard with gusto. Grandma warned me to slow down because the day was young yet. I looked at my grandmother and realized for the first time that she was getting old. She had forgotten how young people had a lot of energy and could outwork older people. At thirteen I was already feeling the coming of manhood. I even had the proof—three whiskers protruding from my chin which I took to stroking when I was deep in thought. I surveyed the yard and thought that maybe it might take a couple of hours of hard work to complete it. I figured we would be done before lunchtime.

With Grandma working next to me, I attacked the dirt with vigor and determination.

"Whoa, slow down there, Geoffrey. You won't last at that rate."

"It's okay, Grandma. I'm all right. It won't take me long. Watch."

In no time I was tired, sweating and grunting as I fought the rake through the soil. I looked at Grandma. She looked as cool and refreshed as when she'd first come outside. She had raked a slightly smaller section than I, but it seemed as if she could rake all day.

"Ready to take a break?" she asked when she saw me looking at her.

She could tell I was exhausted. I'm sure she smiled inwardly at my feigning otherwise. I dropped the rake and stumbled to the back of the house, afraid my arms would never stop hurting. My grandmother brought me a glass of lemonade and words of wisdom at the same time.

"Geoffrey, you know work is a very important thing. And I know a lot of people who don't know how to pace themselves. So they start out real good. I mean they just are going and going. But after a while they start to peter out. And in the end you find out that they wasn't worth two hoots. You have to learn how to size up a job. Remember each job has a beginning, a middle, and an end. You keep worrying about the end. You're trying to get to the end so quick you think you can skip the beginning and the middle—you understand what I'm trying to tell you?"

"Yes, Grandma," I said. But that wasn't exactly the truth. I didn't really understand.

"Let me tell you about work. The first thing you have to do is to size up the job. How long will it take? Then, in the beginning, try to figure out the easiest way to get the job done as quickly as possible. You spend five minutes pulling on an old root when if you chopped it with the hoe you'd be done in five seconds. You see?"

"Yes, Grandma, I see that."

"Good. In the beginning ask yourself, 'How can I do it quicker using less energy?' You experiment a lot until you come up with a system. Then in the middle, which is usually the longest part of the job, you learn to enjoy it. You set a pace and a rhythm and you set your mind to work. Did you know that you can enjoy even hard labor?"

"No, Grandma, I didn't. I don't think I could ever enjoy raking. It's so hard and boring."

"Raking is hard, but sometimes you make a job harder than it is by hating it or fighting it. Work is work. Sometimes it's hard, sometimes it's easy. Let me tell you a secret. When you're doing hard work like this with your body, you can be doing other wonderful things with your mind. That's how you make the pain and boredom go away."

"Grandma, what about the end of the job? You haven't talked about that."

"You have to finish a job with enough energy to make sure the end is done just as well as the beginning. People are often exhausted by the time they reach the end of the job. They start taking short cuts and they can sometimes ruin the whole thing just because they didn't know that the end is as crucial as the beginning. When you take pride in your work, once you've finished a job you can look back at it and know that you've done the best you could. And when that's the case sometimes you can come back years, even decades later and see that your work has remained intact because you did it right from beginning to end."

Raking the yard and removing the debris was only the beginning. Our next task was even more grueling. We had to even out the side of the property line that sloped downward. And with that effort I began to learn my second lesson about working that summer.

The task was simple but would demand great effort. We had to carry dirt from the back of the property to the front and build up the boundary line between my grandparents' land and the adjacent lot. The problem was that the ground was too soft for the wheelbarrow when it was loaded with dirt. So we resorted to carrying the dirt in buckets. We formed a simple assembly line. My grandmother shoveled the dirt with one of my brothers, the others of us carried the dirt in the buckets. I tried to remember what grandma had told me about working because it became apparent real fast that this was not going to be a quick job. Each time we emptied a bucket of dirt we looked to see if we could see any difference in the front yard. We couldn't. In fact, after a whole day of moving dirt, outside of some aching arms and shoulders, some calluses on the hands, we could see no signs we had been at work at all.

That night we all ate a nice big dinner and I wondered how long it would take to finish the yard. I was more tired physically than I had ever been before, but sitting at the table with my brothers and grandparents talking about the work we had done, and the work we still had to do, made me feel proud. I had never been treated as an equal by adults. I felt now that I was really contributing something. More importantly, my grandparents treated me as if I had earned their respect. It wasn't anything big, it was the little things they said that made me feel as if I had just gone through a rite of passage.

"Now, Geoffrey, have some more cornbread. You know you have to replace all that energy you used up today," Grandma said.

"Thanks, Grandma. Don't mind if I do."

"Let me look at those hands. Didn't you say your hands were hurting?" Grandpa asked.

"Yes, Grandpa. Right here," I said, showing him my hands palms up.

"Well now, let me see. You know, it looks like you just growing a few calluses on those hands. That's what hard work will do for a man. They might be sore for a couple of days. It happens to all men who work hard like we do. How do they feel now?" Grandpa asked.

"They don't feel so bad. It's nothing really," I said, feeling that I'd earned the pain that flashed through my sore hands whenever I closed them. I was proud of that pain because I was a working man now.

My brothers and I carried pails of dirt for weeks. It was hard, hot, back-breaking work. We thought we would never finish, but we did. We had a celebration to signal the end—Grandpa cut a watermelon and we took big slices and walked the front yard admiring our work. The ground was now smooth and even all the way to the end of the property line. I wasn't all that happy to see the end of the job. We had become quite a team. Grandma was right, hard work could be fun if you had the right attitude. I was disappointed to know we couldn't plant grass that summer; it was too late. But the next spring we seeded and watched as a lush, green, even lawn sprouted up.

I have had many jobs, many of them menial, since my grandparents taught me how to work. None of those jobs were ever as hard as the work I did for free with my grandparents. This is not the case for too many children today. Boys who think that they are ready for the world, ready to drop out of school at fifteen or sixteen, or at least get it over with, need to learn first about hard work. They need to understand that unless they excel in school, their options will be very limited. They will face fierce competition for the relatively few unskilled jobs that still exist. And many of them will not be properly prepared even for those. They don't have experience with the world of work. They haven't developed good work habits, a positive attitude, or an understanding of what will realistically be required of them.

While we must have high standards when it comes to young people working, we must in the first place create opportunities for them. Simply complaining about youth crime and people on welfare will not solve the problem of how we produce employable adults. Many young people are totally alienated from the world of work because of where they live, or because of the color of their skin. We must level the playing field when it comes to opportunity in this country by making sure that we remove the barriers that so many of our youth face in finding and keeping jobs.

To begin with, it is imperative that we increase the number of jobs available for our youth. And in particular we must focus on creating jobs for the young people who are the most discriminated against—black boys. This responsibility must be borne not only by government, by increasing the job programs that already exist, but also by the corporate, not-for-profit, and small business sectors in America as well. We must find creative ways of drawing huge numbers of boys who presently can't find jobs into the world of work. We might try a tax credit for businesses that hire young people from poor communities, or asking corporations to partner with certain communities in this effort.

Our strategies with young people at Rheedlen are based on the simple idea that work is a key ingredient in keeping young people engaged in school and community. We always have a group of young people around who are employed by us to deliver messages, do maintenance work, and answer the phones. All of the teenagers who work for us have to be enrolled in school and passing their classes, as I said earlier. Failure to do so means a warning first, then termination from the Rheedlen job. We have found this to be a very effective mechanism for making sure young people graduate from high school and develop job skills or go on to college. Many of our young people don't have clear career goals as teenagers, but then again, neither did many of my friends who went on to live productive, successful lives as adults simply because it was expected of us. At Rheedlen we have tried to create an environment that puts the same positive pressure on young people that many of us felt at home as children.

We have tried to make the connection between work and school real for young people at an early age. While teenagers might not have figured out what passing tenth-grade English has to do with being employable later on in life, they know that passing that class has everything to do with keeping a job today. And we have found that the best way to get our young people to go on to college is for everybody to simply expect him or her to do so. So starting in their junior year at high school they begin to field questions from the professional staff at Rheedlen about their plans after graduation. By their senior year everyone at Rheedlen, including the secretarial staff, begins to ask about young people's plans for college. They are harangued about taking the SATs and filling out financial aid forms. When all of the adults around you believe you can do something, like going to college, pretty soon you begin to believe it also. So most of our young people, with help from us, go through the process of applying to college, filling out forms, writing personal statements—and lo and behold, most are accepted somewhere. (If they are accepted to a college in New York City, they usually end up keeping their jobs with Rheedlen, but the same rule applies—they do so only if they are in school.)

My grandfather and grandmother passed away years ago, and the house they built was sold. Every now and then I drive out to Wyandanch, past the house, just to look at it. The maple trees we planted thirty years ago as saplings are now huge trees. The house shows some signs of wear and tear, but the lawn is even. And each time I drive by I remember that the lessons I learned from my grandmother about work were good, honest, universal lessons that all of us need to learn. We should view work, hard work, as a necessary rite of passage for boys early in their lives. We must teach them that there is nothing demeaning in working hard, whether it's for money or not.

And we must rethink our roles in providing jobs for young people. Schools, businesses, government, and private citizens must participate in new ways to provide training, work opportunities, and job mentoring. We know that increasingly in our country jobs require more training and educational experience, higher standards of performance, and the ability to adapt to changing global forces in the labor market. Preparing poor boys in particular to compete in this environment will not be easy. It will call for new strategies and investments of money and our own energy. It will take time. If we are committed and thoughtful—if, like my grandmother taught, we do the best we can from beginning to middle to end—we can make the choices today that will mean that for all boys the lawn will still be even thirty years from now. And we can take pride in a job well done.

Mentors

THE YEAR WAS 1965 and I was thirteen years old. Heroin
was turning what used to be relatively safe neighborhoods in the South Bronx into dangerous, crime-infested
war zones. On Union Avenue, we watched in amazement as boys
we had always admired, even boys who had told us to "leave that
shit alone," became junkies and nodded into a dreamland they
never wanted to come out of. And we watched as in what seemed
like no time at all but was actually several years, the heroin culture changed our sense of community, changed the way we lived.

Union Avenue, like most of the inner-city neighborhoods in
New York, had a tough, sometimes violent, street culture. But
once you crossed the threshold into your apartment, you lived in
relative safety. This was a time when there were no bars on windows, no double and triple locks on doors. Neighbors knew one
another, and everyone knew the children who lived on the block.
People were poor and life was hard, but there still existed a community structure that was strong and vibrant. The heroin epidemic that swept New York and communities like it across this
country, beginning in the early sixties, changed all of that.

We began hearing tales of burglaries. Someone's television would mysteriously disappear from their living room with no suspect except a trusted friend. Then the break-ins started, with people going in any unlocked door, taking anything of value. The number of people who told stories of being robbed began to swell. Behavior and life on the block started to change. People started to lock their doors and windows all the time. Strangers were no longer allowed into the house. Everyone was a suspect until proven innocent. Neighbors began to suspect their neighbors, friends suspected their friends, mothers and fathers suspected their sons and sometimes their daughters. And this suspicion descended on Union Avenue like a dark cloud. People who once smiled at you now looked warily away. Where once you helped bring the groceries of a neighbor into the kitchen, now she stopped you at the doorway with "Thank you, I'll take it from here." The number of break-ins increased, and suddenly people were being robbed in their own hallways and no place seemed safe anymore. As the number of junkies increased, so did the mayhem they caused in their desperate attempts to get money for drugs. Even before the people began to die as the violence increased, the sense of community died first. And the most feared and suspected group, the one most blamed for creating havoc in the community, were teenage boys.

So I came into my teen years as the community began to shun adolescents the way they would a contagious disease. We were not embraced, we were kept at arm's length. At one of the most crucial junctures in our lives, when we desperately needed adult support and guidance, it began to disappear. We were not bad kids and we could see the destruction that heroin was causing in our community. A few of the boys and girls my age were beginning to experiment with heroin, but most of us knew the drug's dangers, had witnessed the slow physical and moral destruction of friends, and had decided not to use it. But just because we didn't experiment with heroin didn't mean that there weren't other vices to tempt our adolescent curiosity.

At thirteen I was at a crossroads in my life. I was old enough and tough enough to begin to explore all the Bronx had to offer. I hung out with a group of boys the same age and we were obsessed with girls, sports, and fighting. We smoked cigarettes and drank Gypsy Rose or Thunderbird, or whatever other cheap wine came into fashion. We knew we represented the next generation of tough boys to "rule on the block." And while we weren't looking for trouble, neither were we running away from it.

We didn't have any relationships with the men on our block, but we, like all boys, desperately wanted to learn how to become men ourselves. Our only male role models were the older boys, and we copied their behavior and attitudes in all ways. So it was a shock to me when three real men came into my life.

It was Ned, one of my best friends, whose family lived downstairs from us on Union Avenue, who told me about the men. Ned's uncle was one of them. He and two friends had decided that black boys needed men in their lives. Men who were stable, sober, with good jobs. Men who would be the role models boys growing up in the South Bronx never had. So they told Ned to invite some of his friends to a new club they were starting. Ned invited me, and, having nothing better to do, I attended my first meeting one Saturday.

There were about twelve of us boys in a small room in a church on Prospect Avenue, which was within walking distance from my apartment building. The first thing I noticed about the three men was that they were not from "around the way," as we called the South Bronx. They were dressed in jackets and ties, white shirts gleaming. I tried to figure out what their con was, what it was they wanted. The one named Reginald seemed the most at ease with us. I decided he would be a good starting place to smoke out their true intentions.

"Okay, I heard you say how you gonna help us poor boys out," I began with intentional coarseness. "How we ain't got no father and shit. So you three, like the Three Musketeers, are coming back to the ghetto, back to where they piss and shit in the hallways, and the junkies knock old ladies in the head for their welfare checks. You three are gonna rescue us from all that shit. Is that what you saying?"

The other boys chuckled at the obvious discomfort I'd caused two of the men. But Reginald was not intimidated by tough talk.

"We're here trying to help," he stated simply. "We can't save the whole world, but we can help save some of you who want to save yourselves. We can't do it for you, but we can help you get it done. We're men. Black men. We grew up just like you. Poor. Living hard. But we worked hard and made something out of our lives. We could have stayed where we live now, but we came back to try to help. We want to try to be your friends."

I sat there looking at the men, listening to Reginald and thinking, "What a load of shit this is. These guys don't know shit about our lives. They think they know but I doubt they could even walk down Union Avenue without getting their ass kicked."

The meeting adjourned and I left, planning never to go back again. A week later, though, Ned talked me into going one more time. At this second meeting it was decided that the name of the club would be GTU, or Growth Through Unity. The men spent much of the meeting talking about hard work and honesty. They saw that many of us were less than enthusiastic. They asked us what we wanted from the club. We said basketball. We were at that age where we loved basketball. We wanted our own team. With uniforms. With sneakers. They said they would do it if we came to weekly tutoring and achievement classes. That's how I became a card-carrying member of GTU.

Over the course of the next few months GTU was to become part of my weekly routine. Reginald was the only one of the men who had a clue about what our lives were really like, but the other two, Donald and Ned's uncle, Jerry, tried hard and were earnest. We went to our classes and they kept their end of the deal, forming a basketball team, getting us uniforms and finally sneakers. After we had attended GTU for about four months they bought each regular member a blue blazer with a GTU patch sewn on the pocket. It was the first blazer I'd ever had, and I had to admit these guys were growing on me.

The wilderness trip, though, put an end to all that. It was doomed from the beginning. And when I caution those who want to volunteer to mentor and work with children to start slow, that good mentors have to have more than just good intentions, it is because I remember this misadventure. What went wrong? Now I realize that the gulf between those of us growing up on the streets of New York City in the sixties and those who had grown up twenty years before us was simply too wide.

We drove up in a van. Our destination, still a secret to us boys, was a small campground in upstate New York. There were about eight of us, all excited about what for many of us would be our first wilderness experience. Our three mentors seemed just as excited as we were. They had been planning this overnight trip for some time. The van ride was about four hours. Our patience lasted about ninety minutes. When I think about it now, I guess the men had decided not to tell us the trip took four hours because they were afraid that if they did we wouldn't want to go. Their refusal to tell us how long we had to travel to reach our destination was the first tactical mistake.

I had taken on the role of one of the leaders in GTU, and I now saw part of my job as being chief complainer for our group.

"Damn, man, when are we going to get to this place? Are we there?"

"Don't curse," Donald answered. "We'll get there when we get there."

" 'Damn' ain't no curse. It's in the Bible. Now, shit and motherfucker—those are curses. I didn't say, "Damn motherfucker where is this piece of shit place?' I just said damn."

"Geoff, why don't you stop playing games. You know the rules of GTU. No cursing. Respect for your elders. Maintain control of yourself. So quit being a wise guy," Jerry said to me.

"Well, I don't know how much respect you all are showing us. We been in this beat-up van for hours and we still don't know where we're going. I guess you think that's respect?"

"It hasn't been hours, it's only been ninety minutes. Why don't you just cool out and look at the scenery. Look. Right over there. See that herd of cows?" Jerry said, trying to change the topic.

Even though for a bunch of city kids cows and horses were an exotic sight, we had already passed several scenes like this, and it kept our attention for only a minute or two. My friend Neddy was sitting next to me, and in a very short time he picked up where I had left off.

"So are we there yet?"

"No," Donald said.

"Well, are we close? Why won't you tell us how much longer it's going to be?"

"You'll know we're there when we're there. Period. End of discussion," Donald said, irritation in his voice. There was a certain challenge, a threat that we heard in the way he made his statement. Boys like us were trained to pick up even the most subtle cues of hostility or threat behavior. If they thought they were going to get us out of our territory and then threaten us, intimidate us, try to take our manhood, we knew we had to stop that right here.

"What d'you mean, 'You'll know we're there when we're there'? What's that supposed to mean?" Ned asked.

"Why can't you answer our questions? We ain't no two-year-olds. For all I know you guys could be kidnapping us," I said, knowing I would either escalate the confrontation, which we would prefer to have right now, or Jerry and Donald would have to back down.

Donald was mad. "Geoff, you're always starting trouble. If you didn't want to follow the rules, why didn't you stay home? We would have been fine without your company."

"Why didn't *you* stay home? Nobody likes you anyway."

The words flew out of my mouth before I had a chance to think about their impact. It was true that of the three mentors, we liked Donald the least. He was the most uptight, the least open to us. And I was at an age where I didn't accept challenges without responding, and often overresponding. In this case I hit a raw nerve. Donald was stung by what I had said and the way I'd said it. I'm sure he'd never had a thirteen-year-old talk to him so rudely before. But he made matters worse.

"Geoff, you're such a smartass. I wish you were my son for one minute. I bet you'd learn to watch what you say then," he said, turning from his seat in the front of the van to look back at me.

"What'd you say? I'm a *what*? Did you say 'ass'?" I said, covering my mouth in mock surprise. "I thought you were here to teach us poor boys how to deal with our emotions without using profanity." The other boys laughed a little nervously. They knew I was angry and capable of saying anything.

"And as for being your son, I would never have no punk-assed father like you. You think you scare me. Stop the van. Stop the motherfucking van! Me and you, Donald. Right here in the motherfucking woods. A fair one—me and you. You don't scare me. Shit, you can't do nothing to me."

I meant what I said. I was taught never to let another man take my manhood away and I felt that was what Donald was attempting to do. And Donald looked soft to me. I thought that in what we considered a fair fight on the street I might hold my own. I didn't have to win the fight, just not lose. That would shame him to no end.

My words angered Donald further. He was not prepared for the insults and the threat. He stood up. "Who do you think you're talking to? You don't know me, boy. I'll wring your neck!"

I stood up too, in the back of the van. "Come on. I dare you. Come back here and try to wring my neck."

Reginald, who knew what I was doing and where this was heading, intervened. He grabbed Donald by the arm and began whispering in his ear. I could see Donald suddenly look at all of the other boys and see their eyes were on him. Watching him, judging him. Reginald took control. "Come on, you guys. We are all part of the same club. Remember? Growth Through Unity. Now we still have another two hours to drive. Let's settle down. Quit complaining. Let's act like brothers. Like men. All right? Geoff—you cool?"

"Sure I'm cool. Forget about it. I'm cool," I answered.

"Donald, you cool?" Reginald asked.

"Yeah, I'm cool," he said, slipping back into his seat.

I was smiling as I sat back down. Reginald had answered the question. We had two hours to go. That should be the end of the men keeping information from us and treating us like kids. Donald was looking back at me. I could see that in our one brief confrontation I had made an enemy. He cut his eyes to see if any of the other kids were watching him. With the drama over, they'd gone back to staring out the window at the never-ending scenery of trees and hills. He looked at me and smiled and nodded his head up and down. His message was clear. This wasn't over. I smiled back at him. I wasn't scared of Donald. I had something he knew nothing about—my K55 knife, right in my back pocket. I knew how to use it and wasn't afraid. Donald might be thinking he could get me off somewhere in the woods and scare me or try to get even. Wouldn't he get the surprise of his life.

After a trip that had seemed interminable, we finally arrived at the camp. The rolling hills were green and lush. The air was fresh and crisp. A stream ran through a little valley near a cluster of cabins. It was a beautiful and secluded campground. I thought to myself that the long trip was worth it, this looked like paradise. Paradise didn't last long.

The first shock was the cabins. They were exactly what our mentors wanted—rustic. We looked more closely at the log cabins and couldn't believe our eyes. The only time any of us had seen a log cabin was in books about Abraham Lincoln. Inside, the cabins were dark and dusty. The bedding on the wood-frame beds had to be taken outside, laid across a line, and beaten with sticks to knock the dust out. The cabins had no lights, no sinks, no bathrooms. The spaces between the logs were large enough to see through.

Two different sets of expectations came crashing together at this moment, in this out-of-the-way setting, with something like the impact of the head-on collision of two locomotives traveling at full speed. The men thought being somewhere where we had to build a fire to eat, cut wood to build a fire, and sleep in log cabins exposed to plenty of fresh air was just the thing we needed to learn self-reliance and teamwork. We thought "camp" meant screened porches, swimming pools, a lounge with a television set, not this beat-up, dusty, isolated place with housing that was even worse than the slums we thought we were escaping for a weekend. We all became depressed and sullen. We griped about having to sweep out the cabins and beat the dust out of the bedding. Many of us looked with alarm at the size of the spiderwebs that hung in every corner of the cabin. Even as we swept the webs away, we wondered where the spiders were and what they would be doing when we tried to go to sleep that evening.

The last of our swagger disappeared when we ran, screaming and waving our arms, from a bumble bee that looked to be the size of a small bird. We were off our turf, frightened of the bugs, and unsure about the sounds of nature all around us. The men laughed at how shaken we seemed at being in the middle of the wilderness. They felt our insecurity was a good thing. They began to tell us things about the birds, the trees, the insects. Our natural curiosity overcame our fear, and we began to appreciate our surroundings and the men who had brought us here. For a while.

We had never seen a snake in the wild before. Donald pointed it out to us from the bank of the stream. "See that over there? There's a snake. See it? Right under that root. There, it's moving. See it?"

We saw it. It was about three feet long. We all were amazed. A snake right there in the water. Only twenty yards from our cabins. Wow!

"That's a water moccasin. Never go near a snake unless you know what type of snake it is," Donald lectured. He could have saved this advice. None of us had any interest in getting near a snake, no matter what kind it was.

"Wait here. I'm going to show you something," Donald said, dashing off to the cabin where the men were staying. He came back with a long canvas bag that he began to unzip. He removed a rifle, and we all took a step toward him.

"Stand back, stand back. Don't crowd. This is a real rifle and you never approach someone who has one of these in his hands unless you know it's not loaded." He checked the gun to make sure it wasn't loaded and then let us gather around to inspect it. None of us had ever seen a real gun before. Donald carefully showed us how to load the rifle. He even let us hold the bullets.

"Watch this." Donald shouldered the gun and pointed it across the riverbank. "See the snake? Watch."

He sighted down the rifle and we heard a loud crack as he fired. We could see his torso rock back smoothly as he absorbed the recoil. We all flinched at the sound of the shot, and we opened our mouths in amazement as we saw the head of the snake pop up and then fall lifeless onto the moist riverbank. The dead snake slowly slid down the bank into the river. The current began to carry it downstream. We all looked from the snake back to Donald. He had a self-satisfied smile on his face. He cradled the rifle, patted it several times, and began to put it back into its canvas bag.

"Can I shoot it?" I asked, completely forgetting Donald's and my recent confrontation.

"No." He responded.

"Why? Why can't we try it?" I really wanted to shoot that rifle. The whole trip would be a success if I could go back on the block and tell the other kids I had shot a rifle.

"Guns are dangerous. Only men should handle guns. All of you are too young to shoot a gun. This ain't no toy." And with that, Donald zipped up the bag and took the gun back into his cabin.

All of us were a little disappointed. But soon I began to develop a new worry. I had felt confident about coming out to this camp in the middle of nowhere because I was armed with my trusty knife. I had no idea that they would have guns. I knew Donald didn't like me and I didn't like him. But now I had to look on him with new respect. He could shoot. He could shoot real well. My concern deepened. The men had never mentioned they would be bringing guns, guns they wouldn't let us shoot or even touch. I had made Donald angry intentionally, now I didn't know if that was such a smart thing I had done. I was ready to use my knife to defend myself if I had to. What if Donald was prepared to use his rifle? This thought bothered me, but for the moment I decided to keep my anxieties to myself.

We were each given chores to help prepare for dinner. Some

had to collect wood for the fire, some had to fill up buckets with water, others had to wash the vegetables. My job was to gather kindling. I walked into the woods and began to pick up small twigs. The deeper I walked, the more ominous the woods seemed to me. I could hear things scampering through the dry leaves, but each time I stood up to see what it was, I saw nothing. I began to remember every story I had ever read in the *National Enquirer* about grizzly bear attacks. Suddenly I lost my nerve, bundled what little kindling I had gathered up, and headed back.

There was nobody else around when I got back. The other boys were still away doing their chores, so I decided to go for a stroll around the campground. As I walked past the men's cabin I could hear them talking.

Jerry was saying, "So first we'll set up the place deep in the woods. We'll need to bring firewood there in advance so we can have a nice fire once we arrive. We have to make sure they don't know what we're up to. I have an idea—let's blindfold them."

When I heard "blindfold," I stopped dead in my tracks. I tip-toed to the side of the cabin and pressed my ear to one of the cracks between the logs. It was Donald who spoke next.

"How are we going to get them to wear blindfolds? You know how they've been acting."

Jerry answered, "We'll tell them we have a special treat for them at a secret campsite. We'll make it seem like it will be real fun. Then we'll put the blindfolds on loose. Even if they pull them down they won't be able to tell which way they're going. It's pitch black out here at night. We'll take them every which-a-way until they're totally confused. Then once we get them there, we'll do it."

I couldn't believe my ears. Thank God I'd only heard Donald and Jerry. Reginald was on our side. He would help us. He was the only one I really trusted. But Donald had the gun. What could Reginald do? Well, we would just have to figure out something. Together with Reginald we could overpower the other two before

Donald could get his rifle. I was about to tiptoe away when I heard a voice that crushed my hope of deliverance.

"Listen, let me talk to them. They trust me." It was Reginald. "Donald, you don't say anything. I'll make it seem like just an innocent game. So, right after dinner . . ."

I had heard enough. I stole away back toward our cabin. I found Neddy first.

"Get all the boys together. I got to talk to everybody. Now! Come on. Tell them to meet me behind our cabin. Get everybody."

Neddy looked at me strangely, but off he dashed. It took about fifteen minutes to gather up all the boys from their different work assignments. They looked somewhat confused and disoriented. The different smells, noises, and configuration of the country were starting to take their toll. I called them over and they formed into a semicircle. I knelt down and they did the same thing. They could tell by the way I kept looking around me that something important was going on. Ned asked what was on everybody's mind.

"What's up, Geoff?"

"I think we got a problem," I answered, keeping my voice low. "I was walking over by the men's cabin and I heard something I think you should know."

I had everyone's attention. This group knew that I was not prone to lying or exaggeration. They knew that I lived on one of the toughest blocks in the South Bronx and that I always carried a knife and wasn't afraid to use it. So if I thought we had a problem, they were willing to accept that as a fact.

"They plan to come for us tonight. They're going to blindfold us, tie our hands, and take us into the woods and do something to us."

I realized as I spoke that I hadn't actually heard the men mention tying our hands. I assumed that this is what they planned to

do, because it was inconceivable to me that they would think we'd
go meekly off to our demise without putting up a fight. To keep us
from fighting they would have to tie our hands. I intentionally
used the phrase "do something to us." The boys could not help but
think of the most ominous meaning. Our young lives already had
witnessed many acts of horror and brutality. Many of these acts
were committed by men. Our minds raced over the different negative experiences that we'd had or heard about involving men. For
Neddy and me there were many episodes to consider. One of our
worst fears involved what we had heard about homosexual rape.

In the late fifties, several of the leaders of the Disciples, the gang
that ruled our area of the Bronx, had been arrested as part of a
crackdown on gangs, and sent away to jail. They were still in jail
when my family moved onto Union Avenue. After being on the
block for about a year, I thought I knew all the important older
boys, and I was surprised when several of those who had been arrested began coming back. The first thing I noticed was that they
got instant respect from everyone. These guys were really tough.
On our block they were at the top of the pecking order, and all of
us hoped that one day we could be as tough, as fearless. One day
two of the boys who had done a couple of years upstate in the
penitentiary began to talk to us. Both Ronald and Sam had been
respected members of the Disciples; Ronald had been war coun-
selor for the gang.

"Listen, when you go to jail, don't take shit from nobody," Ronald began.

I was immediately stunned. Ronald didn't say *if* you go to jail,
he said *when*. It was clear to me that he expected all of us to go to
jail one day. I wondered why we all had to go.

"That's right," Sam chimed in. "Don't take no cigarettes, no
candy bars, no nothing. If you ain't got no money, fuck it. Do
without. Be a man."

"And when they try to make a move on you," Ronald continued, "fuck them up. I mean fuck them up good. Not with your hands. Pick up something, a tray, a stool, anything you can get your hands on. Don't say nothing. Just bust them upside their fucking head. Try to tear their fucking head off. Yell and scream and shit like you a madman. Let everybody know you ain't afraid to kill a motherfucker."

While he was saying this Ronald's face took on a crazed look. We all stepped back, not knowing what he might do. Sam was shaking his head in agreement as Ronald was talking. All of us were staring at the two of them, transfixed. These were the toughest guys in the whole world, and they were talking about guys who would try to bother *them*? Who would be crazy enough to bother Sam and Ronald? And why? I could see from the looks of confusion on the other boys' faces that they were thinking the same thing I was, but were trying to play hip. Since I was the youngest, I knew I shouldn't be the one to ask the question, but I felt that the two gang members had been telling us this for a reason that was part of our education on the streets of the South Bronx. And one day, according to them, we would all be in jail. I wanted to be prepared.

So I asked, "Why shouldn't you take candy bars? And if anybody messes with you why don't you just beat them up like you do around here?"

The other boys were both amazed and relieved that I'd had the nerve to ask Ronald and Sam the things we all were wondering. And from what happened next they knew they had been smart to keep their mouths shut.

"Who asked that dumbass shit?" Ronald scanned us quickly with eyes that were cold and unblinking. His eyes fell on me and my legs got weak.

"Come here, little nigger. Did you ask that dumb shit? What's your name?"

"My name's G—G—Geoffrey," I stammered, wondering why God had given me such a big mouth.

"Come here," he snarled. I couldn't move. "Didn't you hear me call you? Then get the fuck over here."

I staggered over wondering what I had gotten myself into. I stopped about three feet from Ronald. "Yes," I managed to say.

"Not over there, nigger, over here. Right here," Ronald said, pointing to a spot only six inches from where he was standing. I looked at the spot, blinking my eyes, trying to stay calm. Ronald was known to be a dangerous guy with a bad temper if you made him mad. I walked over to him feeling as if I was in a pirate movie, walking the plank.

"Now what do you think those guys who are locked up for thirty years want with nice young, tender, pretty boys like us?" he asked, looking anything but young, tender, or pretty. As he said this Ronald was caressing my face in a way that was repulsive to me. And even though I was terrified of him, I couldn't help but pull my head back and away from his touch.

"Well, what do you think?" Ronald screamed in my face.

When he yelled I flinched and put up my hands, fists balled up, more out of reflex than anything else.

"Nigger, don't you put your hands up to me. I'll punch you in your fucking face. Put your hands down." Ronald was furious. I could see he was losing control. I put my hands down as quickly as possible. He shook his head, not believing I'd had the gall to raise my fists to him. He kept twisting his head from side to side, looking back to me then off to the side over his right shoulder, then back to me. I saw him decide. Even though I came only up to his chest and was six or seven years his junior, he was going to punch me. I closed my eyes. It was Sam who saved me. He grabbed Ronald's arm.

"You scairt the little nigger, that's all. He wasn't going to fight you. Be cool, Ronald. Be cool, man. He just a little motherfucker. He don't even know who you are."

Ronald seemed to accept Sam's explanation because when I opened my eyes Ronald was looking at me and smiling.

"You want to know why they give you those cigarettes and candy bars for free? Want to know why those guys try to make a move on you? Turn around."

Ronald wasn't the type of guy I wanted to turn my back on, but I turned, knowing that I had escaped being punched only by Sam's intervention. The pain when it came was unexpected. I fully expected to be slapped in the back of my head. The smack was on my behind. The force of it lifted me off the ground a couple of inches. The sound of Ronald's palm hitting my buttocks was like a pistol shot. The pain felt as if someone had lit a book of matches and thrown them in my underwear. I tried to take it like a man but I couldn't help dancing a little jig and rubbing the spot where I had been smacked. I was worried about what the other boys would be thinking about my not being able to take a smack without acting like a baby, but then I realized none of them was looking at me, they were all looking at Ronald. I could now hear him snarling at us.

"Because they want your ass. They want to fuck you in your ass. They want to take their big dicks," and while saying this Ronald reached down with both hands to the front of his pants and made as if he was holding a penis six inches in circumference, "and they want to shove it up your ass." And as he said "shove," he thrust his pelvis toward us while holding this huge imaginary penis in his hands. All of our eyes were on it. We all involuntarily took two steps away. I jumped back, lost my footing, and fell backward onto the boys behind me. I scrambled back up to my feet, afraid I might have to run for my life. The things he was saying were unimaginable to us.

"They gonna take their big dicks and bust your asshole wide open. Then when they finished they gonna get their friends. Pretty soon everybody be fucking you. You gonna let some big motherfucker put their dick up your ass?" Ronald asked the group.

The boys were outraged. They had forgotten all about me. They couldn't believe someone would try to take your manhood in such a horrid way. They yelled back to Ronald.

"Naw, man. I'll die first."

"I'll kill a motherfucker. Ain't nobody fucking me."

"Let'em try it. The motherfuckers. Let'em try it."

Ronald continued, "And what are you gonna do if someone comes up to you and tells you you look cute? Or winks their eye at you-all?"

The boys couldn't wait to answer.

"I'm gonna pick something up and bust him upside his head."

"I'm gonna try to kill the motherfucker if he even looks at me wrong."

"I'm gonna grab whatever I can get my hands on and then go crazy. They gonna have to pull me off the motherfucker."

Ronald and Sam looked us up and down. They saw that the boys were not playing. The lesson had been hard, but so is life behind bars. Ronald and Sam were not compassionate men, they didn't do what is conventionally considered to be public service work. What they knew they learned from the hard streets of New York City. When they were in a charitable mood they passed on to us what they considered essential for our survival. Having performed their act of charity for the month, they left to go on to some new adventure that we were not invited to attend.

We spent the rest of the afternoon trying to make sense out of what they had told us. How could anyone mistake Ronald or Sam for the kind of guy who might be intimidated into allowing himself to be raped? I mean just one look at them and it was clear that

they were two of the toughest guys in the South Bronx. What kind
of men were there in jail who thought they could rape those two?
It was Mike we went to for the answers.

Mike was older than the rest of us. He was as tough as anyone
on Union Avenue, but he made it his business to counsel us in the
ways of the street and he was not apt to be cruel or mean when he
talked to us. When we needed to more fully understand something that was told to us, we went to Mike. I had the best relationship with Mike of any of us and knew that I could ask him anything without his laughing at me. We found Mike hanging on a
stoop near 168th Street, bouncing a basketball.

"Mike, we was talking with Ronald and Sam and they told us
some junk about the guys in jail trying to . . . trying to . . . take
their manhood. You know what I mean?" I asked.

"Yeah. So they told you, huh?" Mike answered, nonplussed.

"Yeah. They said they even tried to do it to them. Now that ain't
true. Everybody know Sam and Ronald are two of the baddest
dudes on the block."

"Yeah, it's true."

"But I seen Ronald kick Alfred's ass right there on 167th Street.
And Alfred was supposed to be tougher than a motherfucker.
And everybody was out there and saw Ronald just kick his ass.
You mean to tell me they gonna mess with someone with a rep
like that in jail?"

"Let me tell you something. If you a young blood, your rep on
the streets don't mean shit in prison. You got guys in prison that
been there since before you were born. They ain't heard shit about
you. Don't nobody care if you kicked Alfred's ass or anyone else's.
Prison is a different world. Once you go behind those bars you
start all over."

"Yeah, but if you can fight, why can't you just have a fair one?
You know, one on one like we do on the block?"

"Every man go to prison gonna fight. The issue is not whether you gonna fight or not. The issue is whether you afraid to die. You got guys in prison doing thirty years, forty years, life. You know what it's like to be in jail and you're twenty-six and looking at thirty years? You forget about how things was out here. You change. You learn to survive in prison. It's not about fighting. You got guys in there will kill you over a pack of cigarettes, and nobody don't give a fuck. Not the other inmates, not the guards—nobody. You around all these men who don't want to be there, sexually frustrated, angry, ready to explode over the slightest thing. Then you have the booty bandits."

We all leaned in closer. "The booty bandits. Who are the booty bandits?" I asked.

"Some guys in jail are 'stuff.' You know what I mean? They like men. They come to jail that way. Some guys are turned into stuff. It's the booty bandits who break down men, rape them, and turn them out. They do this mostly to young guys who come to prison for the first time and don't know the score."

"Well, how do they do it?" I asked.

"It's simple. They been in jail for years. They know that no matter how tough you were on the streets, the first time you come to jail you're scared. The noise, the bars, the fights—it all fucks you up. You don't know what to do, what's gonna happen next. You don't know the rules. And knowing the rules is the only thing that can save you. What booty bandits do is take advantage of the new guys. They come sit next to you at meals and try to be your friend. They offer you cigarettes and candy bars. The new guys are lonely. They don't have no money, no friends. So the bandits start acting like your big brother, you know? They start saying call them if anybody tries to bother you. That kind of shit.

"What the new guy doesn't know is that in prison you never get something without giving something back. And you always fight your own battles. Those are the rules. But the new guy thinks he got a friend. So he takes a couple of packs of cigarettes over the weeks, and when somebody tries to take his dessert his new buddy stands up and tells the guy to leave him alone, he's with him. Now what the new guy isn't understanding is that all of the guys who been serving time in prison know the score. They know that this guy is being turned out. So when the booty bandit stops someone else from taking the guy's dessert, it's a declaration that this is my new bitch. Anybody that fucks with her got to fight me. Nobody else is allowed to take her off. So now the whole prison knows that the new guy is a punk. Everybody but the new guy.

"So after the new guy is into his friend for a couple of cartons of cigarettes, his new friend comes and asks him for his money or to replace the cigarettes. Well, the new guy doesn't have any money. And the bandit tells him, 'Give me my money or something of equal value.' The new guy doesn't have shit to offer. The bandit tells him, 'Oh, so you take my shit and then don't want to pay me back. What're you trying to do, play me for a punk? You think I'm your bitch? I ain't no bitch and if you don't have my money in a week, you're dead.'"

We were all enthralled. So this is what Sam and Ronald were trying to warn us about. Mike continued.

"So now the guy doesn't know what to do. His only friend in prison has turned on him. The other inmates are all looking at him and shaking their heads, like they know what's going on. When he goes to someone he trusts and asks what he can do, the reaction is not sympathetic. Instead he's told, 'You took his cigarettes. You let him fight for you. Now you gonna give him what he wants. He has every right to come after you. Even try to kill you. You don't take a man's stuff without paying him back.'

"The guy doesn't threaten to rape you right away. Naw, they're smarter than that. Almost any man will fight real hard to keep that from happening. They let fear work on you for a while. You have no friends. Every second you're awake you worry about being jumped. You can't sleep well at night. All the other men begin to look at you funny, like it's already happened. You hear that guys are fighting over you to see who's gonna get you next. The pressure builds day after day. And all the while you see people getting jumped and stabbed and killed, and nobody don't give a fuck. Some people can't take pressure like that. They fold. Those who do are robbed, raped, used as servants, and generally disrespected.

"To make it inside the joint you have to be tough not only physically, but up here." Mike pointed to his head. "What the booty bandits know is that under extreme pressure even the baddest dude can crack. And if you crack they are all over you like vultures. That's why you can't fuck around waiting for shit to go down. You got to get the motherfucker first. If you wait and let somebody scheme on you, sooner or later they gonna get you. They don't come by themselves. They come in bunches. Some hold you down while the others take chances raping you. There's nothing you can do. That's why you can't wait. If someone's out to get you, get him first. Catch him in the yard, or at chow, and try to beat the shit out of him. Try to kill him. That's the only way you get respect in the joint. You got that?"

We nodded our heads yes. We never knew a world existed that was tougher than the streets of the South Bronx. The scene Mike had described was one all of us knew we were not prepared for. Mike could see that we were shaken. He tried to bring his lesson back home to the reality he knew confronted most of us.

"Look, the most important thing in life is that you never let nobody take your manhood. Don't take no shit from no one. There are a lot of people out here looking to see if you're soft. If you'll break under pressure. That's why sometimes we're so hard on you-all. You may be young but you better learn now—don't let nobody take advantage of you. Don't let nobody put you in a situation where you can't act like a man. You got it?"

We got it. The knowledge of what awaited those boys who couldn't act like a man had been seared into our consciousness. Now we finally understood why the older guys were so unforgiving. Now we knew why, when they came out of jail, some proudly strolled up and down the block, and some we never saw again. We had all been made to see a vision of life that for adolescent boys was hell. Men after you, grabbing you, raping you. Fighting back to no avail. Your body and your mind torn, never to be put back together again. And the only protection was to get hard, to get mean, to be ready to fight, kill, and even die to protect your manhood. We heard and understood. And we all became more suspicious of the good intentions of anyone, especially men, and more prepared to fight for the smallest slight of what we considered our manhood.

It was this understanding of the world and the evil it contained that now shaped our thinking in the wilderness in upstate New York. The more we began to think about the supposed camping trip, the more suspicious we became. We had been taught that men didn't act altruistically. That in the end there was an awful price to pay. And now we found ourselves in the woods, with no telephone, no way to call for help. And even more scary to us, nobody knew where we were. We'd told our parents that we were going camping somewhere upstate, but that our actual destination was all a big secret. If something happened, if we were assaulted, raped, and then killed by these men, our bodies might never be found.

As the realization of our predicament set in, we realized that we had disobeyed one of the key tenets of the street. We had trusted strange men. How stupid could we be? Wasn't this exactly the same scenario that Mike had explained to us? We had accepted their kindness; we'd each taken sneakers and a jacket from them. Now it was payback time. And even though there were more of us than them, they had a gun. They also had a plan to blindfold and incapacitate us. I had to act to save the group. I was the one every-body trusted to have good street sense. I should have known bet-ter. But we wouldn't go obediently like sheep to whatever the men had planned. No way.

"Listen, I don't know about the rest of you, but there is no way I'm gonna sit around here and just wait for those guys to come with their guns and tie me up and blindfold me. We gotta make a break for it."

Phillip, a quiet boy, responded, "And go where? Even if we made it to the highway and tried to flag down a car, who's to say they gonna stop? Did you see any black people when we were coming out here? You think some white guy is gonna pick all of us up? Don't make me laugh. Anybody saw us on the road would probably shoot us quicker than Donald and them. We in the mid-dle of the woods. Ain't no street lights. Where we gonna go?"

I looked at Phillip. I realized that he was one of those guys the booty bandits would come gunning for. He was too willing to give up. But not me.

"I don't care. I ain't staying here. If they wanna get me, they gonna have to kill me. I'm gonna hide in the woods."

Neddy looked undecided. "Where we gonna hide? What we gonna do? You know they gonna come looking for us."

"Yeah, I know," I answered. "We're gonna hide down there." I pointed to the ravine where the small stream bisected the camp. "See all that brush and shit? We'll hide right there."

"But that's where they shot the snake. I ain't going down there," Phillip said.

"I know that's where they shot the snake. They know we were

afraid of the snake. They'll never think of looking for us down there. They'll go into the woods thinking that's where we hid. This way we can stay real close to the camp and not get lost. We'll be able to hear what they say if they stand over here and talk."

The group pondered my idea. While it made some sense, no one wanted to go anywhere close to where a water moccasin might be slithering. We knew we had to decide fast, and everyone began to put in their two cents' worth.

"Well, I say we go into the woods. I ain't fucking with no snakes. I'm scairt of snakes."

"Like the woods are gonna be safe. What about lions and tigers and shit like that?"

"This ain't Africa, nigger. Ain't no lions and tigers live in New York."

"Well, what about bears? I bet there are bears out there. I ain't fucking with no bear."

"There ain't no bears here, nigger. You crazy?"

"Well, there might be bears. Ain't no grizzly bears, but there might be some small black bears out there. But they scared of people. I think. I read that in *Reader's Digest*."

"Well, what about wolves? Don't tell me there ain't no wolves out there. I seen one when I was looking for firewood."

"You a lying motherfucker. You ain't seen no wolf."

"Then what'd I see? You so smart. You tell me what I saw. It was this big gray thing with small eyes. It was looking right at me. If that ain't no wolf then what was it?"

"It was probably your mama checking up on you."

"Come on, man, this ain't no time to be fucking around. This shit is serious. Okay, down toward the stream or in the woods? Let's vote."

The talk of bears and wolves had convinced most of the boys that hiding close to the camp was our best bet. As the sun set behind the oak and pine trees we snuck in single file around our log cabin and down toward the stream. We looked for cover behind small bushes that grew along the bank and waited. We didn't have to wait long. Just as the sun set the men came looking for us.

From where we were hiding we could make out some of what the men were saying as they pondered where we were. We caught their conversation in snatches as the wind carried their voices down to us. Sometimes they whispered among themselves, sometimes they yelled our names into the night. When they came right to the edge of the ravine where we were hiding, we thought we would be captured. We all froze. But the dark night, the thick brush, and the fact that the men didn't really think we would hide where we'd seen a snake made their search there more cursory than it might have been. After several minutes we could hear them heading away from us into the woods. They were still yelling our names. We were delighted that our plan was working.

Once we knew the men had left, a whispered debate began again. Some of the boys thought we had overreacted. They felt that the men sounded really concerned about us and that we should come out of our hiding place. I was still against it. A couple of the boys said they were going back to the camp. It was hard to argue with them since we were all miserable. The ground was wet and muddy, we could hear things crawling through the leaves, and strange sounds came from all around us. I began to lose my enthusiasm for hiding, and the steam that had fueled my belief in the evil of men began to leak from my body into the cold, damp earth. Finally I had had enough. I stood up to go back, and the others did too. The sound of men crashing through the woods, though, made us all stand as still as frightened deer. We all dropped back into our hiding places. The men sounded angry and dangerous. This did not sound like a good time to surrender.

The men were indeed angry. They had searched through the

woods for us to no avail. They all were wondering how a nice innocent camping trip had turned into such a disaster. The area
they had decided to bring us to was isolated and vast. If we had
wandered off and become lost we might not be found for days, if
ever. They had debated in the woods while searching for us
whether we were lost or hiding. They couldn't imagine all of us
getting lost at the same time. But if we weren't lost, then why
would we be hiding from them? As the men came back to camp
this was exactly what they were discussing.

"Why? I'll tell you why," Donald hissed through clenched teeth.
"Because they are a bunch of ungrateful, ignorant knuckleheads.
I don't know how I let you-all talk me into this. Wait'll I get my
hands on them."

Reginald answered, "Maybe they heard about the plan and
got scared."

"They couldn't have. They just messing with us. They're somewhere real close. I can feel it," Donald said.

"Yeah, I think Donald's right," Jerry said. "They're not lost. I
bet they're real close by. Those boys aren't stupid. They're not going to go running through the woods in the dark. They're hiding
from us. Let's make them come in."

"Hey, guys! Quit fooling around. Come back here now!" Donald yelled.

"We mean it. We're not playing around with you guys any
more. If you don't come in right now, we're going to come out
there and drag you back. I'm not kidding," Jerry called.

It was Reginald who finally got to us. "Come on, guys. Don't be
scared. We're not gonna be mad. Just come on back. You guys hear
me? Just come back in. Everything's okay. Come on, fellas, it's
dangerous out there in the dark. One of you might really get lost
or hurt. You hear?"

We heard. Neddy, who was closest to me, kicked my leg.

"Let's go back," he whispered. "They're not going to hurt us. You hear Reginald. I'm going back."

I could feel the rest of the boys wanting to go back also. Neddy stood up. So did the others. Finally I did too and we began to crawl hand over hand up the embankment. It was Donald who changed everything. We all heard him say it. "I've had enough of this. You-all keep calling—I'm getting the rifle."

As one we turned and stumbled back to our hiding places. We no longer cared about being quiet. We wanted to find safety. Reginald and Jerry could hear us slipping and sliding through the wet underbrush. Then all kinds of madness broke out.

"They're down there! They're down there!" Jerry yelled.

"Where? Can you see them?" Reginald asked.

"No, but listen. They're down by the river."

"All right. We see you guys. Cut it out. Get your butts up here now."

Craack. The rifle shot sounded through the night.

Reginald, Jerry, and I began to scream at the same time.

"Oh shit! They're shooting at us!" I yelled. "Run for your lives! Every man for himself!"

"Donald, we found them! We found them! It's all right!" Reginald and Jerry yelled to Donald. But Donald's ears were still ringing from the rifle shot, and he couldn't hear them. He fired into the air again. *Craack.*

We began to run as best we could along the steep embankment, parallel to the river. One of the boys tripped and fell just as the third rifle shot went off. He hit the ground with an audible thud and cried out in pain.

"They shot Clarence! They shot Clarence!" I yelled, while stumbling blindly through the dark night. Little did I know that it was an exposed root that dropped Clarence, not a bullet. We left Clarence where he fell. We ran tripping and clutching at the slender vegetation, trying not to slip down the bank into the stream. After about fifty yards we came to a small depression in the riverbank. A small stand of spindly pine trees provided natural cover from anyone looking from above. We all ran full speed and dived into our new hiding place. Lying on our stomachs, we looked up the bank, listening for the men.

We were too far away to hear them clearly any more. Their voices floated disembodied through the summer night, reaching us as partial phrases. We could tell they were arguing but we didn't know what they were arguing about. If we had been close enough to hear, we would have known that Reginald and Jerry were angry at Donald for firing the rifle. Donald had fired to signal us and let us know where the camp was. He'd shot into the air just in case we had really gotten lost, so we might follow the sound of the rifle back to camp. Now they were deciding what to do next.

"We should go get them," Jerry said.

"They'll just run from us. We might scare them too bad, and what if they fall into the river? I don't even know if any of them can swim," Reginald reasoned.

"One of us could move behind them to flush them toward the other two," Jerry countered.

"No, there are too many of them. We don't have to do nothing," Donald said with confidence. "They'll be back here in an hour or two."

"What do you mean? We can't leave those boys out there by themselves," Jerry said.

"I've been here in the summer before. These are city boys. Trust me, they'll be back," Donald said.

The men began to whisper to themselves, and then to laugh. Their laughter filled the air. We could hear it clearly from where we were hiding.

"What's so funny?" Neddy asked, slapping at his neck where something was biting him.

"I don't know," I said. Something that felt like a pinprick made me slap my biceps. We stopped talking when we heard someone whispering in the night.

"Hey, guys. Where are you? Guys. You over there?" It was Clarence.

We were jubilant. Clarence wasn't shot after all.

"You guys left me. I can't believe you left me." Clarence limped over to our hiding place and carefully lowered himself down to the ground.

"We thought you were dead, man. We was out of there. You heard me say 'Every man for himself.' You okay?"

"I fell over something and sprained my ankle. I can barely walk. You guys just left me for dead? I thought you were my—er, Geoff, you got something on your face," Clarence said.

"What *are* these fucking things?" I said, smacking at my cheek.

"They're mosquitoes," Neddy said as he jerked his head away from one buzzing in his ear, then smacked one side of his neck with one hand and the other side of his neck with the other.

"Oh shit! Look!" Clarence said, pointing out toward the stream where the half-moon created a streak of white light that rippled on the water. We strained our eyes, at first seeing nothing, then threw our heads back in amazement as we saw what Clarence was pointing at. Mosquitoes. Thousands of them. Millions of them. All rising up from the still pools of water that collected by the stream. As they rose they came together in a great cloud and hovered as if looking. As if looking for any warm-blooded animal stupid enough to be out at night without proper covering or repellent. To our amazement they rose higher in the air. Then all at once they seemed to charge.

We saw them coming and didn't know what to do. They attacked from all angles at once. The mosquitoes swarmed around our heads, getting into our ears and noses, and if we opened our mouths we had to spit out mosquitoes. It was a fierce battle that didn't last long. Donald was right, there was no way we could stay in those woods at night. There was something in the woods more frightening than poisonous snakes, or bears, or even being shot—hungry mosquitoes.

"Run for your lives! Every man for himself!" I yelled for the second time that evening. We charged straight up the bank of the river.

"Wait for me! Wait for me!" Clarence wailed as we deserted him once again.

The farther we moved away from the river the less intense the mosquito attack became. Finally, as we got closer to the camp, there were only five or ten mosquitoes attacking each one of us instead of the hundreds we had run from. We snuck back into camp using trees and the cover of night as camouflage. We didn't see any sign of the men. When we arrived at our cabin we saw that someone had left us a treasure—two cans of mosquito repellent. We bathed in the stuff. The mosquitoes seemed to find it mildly offensive, although several continued to buzz in our ears and alight on our bodies anyway. We ended up getting in our bunks, huddling under the blankets to ward off our tiny torturers.

One by one the others drifted off to sleep. I was one of the few boys awake when the cabin door opened and Reginald poked his head in to make sure we had come back. He smiled to himself, then saw me looking at him. He shook his head in disappointment and closed the door.

"Yeah—well, fuck you too, Reginald," I muttered as I tried to scratch seven different places at the same time and wondered how the others could sleep after nearly being eaten alive.

The next morning we awoke, cold and covered with itching bites. The men tried to reinvent the spirit of the weekend, but we had no enthusiasm for the day's activities and kept asking what time we were leaving to go home. They explained to us that the night before they'd been planning only a harmless initiation rite—that we'd been in no danger, that the rifle shots were to guide us back to the camp if we were lost. It didn't matter. The fragile trust that had developed between us and the men had been broken.

The trip back to the South Bronx was a quiet one. Most of us slept the entire time. When we arrived back in our neighborhood we boys shook hands with Reginald and Jerry and Donald, and promised to make the next meeting, scheduled for Tuesday evening. Even as we said goodbye, most of us knew we would not come back. The gulf between us and the men, already wide when they came into our lives, had suddenly become a canyon that we didn't have enough energy or faith to find a way to cross. We walked away from them that day feeling safe on our own side, where we at least knew the rules and dangers. The three men disappeared from our lives and were not replaced by other men trying to influence the lives of young boys.

If we are to save the next generation of young boys, they need to be connected to men so that they see examples of the possible futures they might live out as adults. At the same time, we have to be careful that we do not go charging into children's lives without being properly prepared for the different way they see the world. It's as much an issue of class and culture as of race.

This is not a call for people not to get involved in mentoring, but just the opposite. I think all of us must do more to help children at risk, especially our boys. Mentoring is a critical activity that can help support children and can make the difference between a child succeeding or failing. It is my belief that the most powerful force in a child's life is a caring adult and that we must get involved personally if we are going to change the outcomes for those children who face the most difficulties. But unless we are already trained to work with children, we must start slowly. We must understand that children growing up in impoverished circumstances often have a worldview difficult for some adults to comprehend but totally consistent with their life experience. We must spend time understanding what the children with whom we want to work are going through and living with every day.

If this is not understood and factored into our work with children, we can easily create situations that do more harm than good. The gap between the poor and the non-poor, regardless of race, is growing ever larger in this country. Things many of us take for granted—safety, enough food, decent housing, a trip to the movies—poor children may have to struggle to obtain. This often creates circumstances where conflicts and hurt feelings between children and well-intentioned outsiders occur unintentionally.

I have known so many people who want to do good but are not well prepared to work with those they want to help. As any of us who have raised children know, it takes more than love and good intentions to do a good job. There are certain very concrete skills that are necessary in order to work with children. We need to know something about child development, about cultural differences, about the difficulties families face raising children in poverty. This information can be collected from many sources, including local community-based organizations, faith institutions, community leaders, and the children and families themselves.

The sad fact is that in America we have so many poor children of all races who are experiencing similar horrid circumstances in their young lives. We have millions of poor children growing up in homes with single parents who are unable to properly support them, in communities where violence is the norm and not the exception, in schools that have long ago given up on educating them. When people think about volunteering to help children, they often think about the most at-risk children. They fail to realize that there is a much larger population of children who are falling through the cracks more gradually, sometimes less dramatically, and that with a helping hand—some attention, some support, some love—from a caring adult, these children could achieve dramatically better outcomes. There are enough children who need our help that each one of us can find the right match, very likely close to home, and go to work to build trust and offer support in order to make a real difference in the life of a child.

Epilogue

I KNEW ONE of the boys I consider to be my son, Roland, was having a difficult time, and I wasn't happy about having to be away from New York for a long-planned meeting in Maine. I worry about Ronald more than I do about my other sons, because I know he has had the hardest life in many ways. He grew up the poorest, with the least love. He has had no contact with his father, and no other male support in his life except for me. I do what I can, but I know it's not enough. The scars from being badly hurt as a young boy have never healed all the way. He's one of those young men who presents an icy exterior, and to someone who doesn't know better he seems to have no feelings. But sometimes when we talk, the hurt is so near the surface it comes pouring out. Then he gets scared that his strong feelings will drown him and all who are close to him, so he has learned to keep himself closed off to the world and his feelings pushed deep down.

I knew Roland had experienced a couple of major setbacks in his life recently. We had spent quite a bit of time talking about his problems and I'd decided that for the moment he was managing.

So I went off to Bowdoin College, to attend a board of trustees meeting. It was on the last day of the meeting that my wife, Yvonne, called to tell me that she had just heard that Roland was in the hospital, that he had tried to commit suicide. It's strange what you think when you hear news like that. My first thought was "Of all the times to try to commit suicide, why would he have to do it when I'm in Maine and don't know if I can get home?"

The East Coast was having a terrible rainstorm and I didn't know if the airports in New York would remain open. It was a miracle that I was able to get a flight in Portland, but after a rough ride I finally landed at La Guardia Airport. I caught a taxi home and told Yvonne I was going to drive from our apartment in Queens into Manhattan to see Roland. Yvonne warned me that because of the storm the roads were flooded in places and cautioned me to be careful. I told her I'd have no problem. I was wrong.

The trip into the city was a nightmare. There were cars all along the side of the road, conked out because of the rain. Water was standing up to two feet deep in some places, and as I drove the rain only grew in intensity. A trip that usually takes me only forty minutes took two hours. I finally arrived, double-parked on the street, and knocked on Roland's door. His mother opened it and I could see the shock on her face and Roland's as I stood there dripping wet from the storm. I hadn't expected to see Roland. I'd come to his apartment to ask his mother what hospital he was in. I was furious to find out that the hospital had already released him; I knew this was because he was poor and without insurance.

"Get dressed and come with me to my car. I want to talk to you," I said.

Roland looked at his mother, then back at me. I knew he was trying to figure out whether or not I was mad at him. His mother looked relieved to see me there. This wasn't the first time I had shown up at her door during a crisis. Roland and I went out into the deserted street in the pouring rain. Once we were seated—both soaked now—in the front seat of the car I asked, "Why didn't you call me?"

"Brian told me you were out of town," he answered, not looking at me.

"You have my pager number. Why didn't you page me?"

"I forgot to tell you that I lost it. I had the number with some papers and I can't find it now. Anyhow, I know how busy you are."

"I got here as soon as I could. I'm glad it wasn't too late. Let me say something."

"What?"

"I'm *never* too busy for you if you need to see me. You understand? You're my son and I love you. Do you understand that I love you?"

He nodded his head yes.

"Now tell me what's hurting you so bad that you couldn't tell your old man. Your father's getting too old to be out driving in rainstorms. Next time have a little consideration. Check the weather first before trying to commit suicide. Okay?"

Roland looked at me. Then the smile that I adore crept across his face as he realized I was joking. And in a double-parked car on a stormy night, we talked about the pain that haunted him every day, about the dreams that had evaporated into the mist of a cold reality, about the rage that stormed across his soul seemingly from nowhere. And we talked about the worst feeling of all for him—of being alone. Alone and cut off from any source of protection or security. So alone that nobody else would understand, could understand.

When the talking was done, when we had bared our souls and shared with one another what we needed to share to begin the healing, we got out of the car. As I watched Roland walk across the street back to his apartment building he looked so small and so alone. And I remembered when he'd been a little boy and I'd watch him go into the same building on the same block. The time had passed too quickly. I hadn't done enough.

"Roland, wait a minute," I yelled, running across the street.

He turned toward me as I tried to jump over a puddle that was in danger of turning into a small pond. I didn't quite clear the water and I could feel the cold pouring into my shoe.

"Not long ago I would have made that jump with no problem. Your dad is getting old." Roland looked at me as if for the first time. I could see him realizing that he could have cleared that puddle easily, that what I'd said was true. I was getting old and he realized with sadness, like all children do, that one day, like all parents, I would not be there for him.

"Come here and give me a hug," I said.

He came into my embrace, and I turned his head into my shoulder and hugged him tight. I hugged him the way all little boys need to be hugged, the way I once hoped my father would hug me. He became embarrassed being hugged this way on the street, where any of his friends might suddenly come upon us. But I didn't care. I didn't let go. So what if he's embarrassed? That's what fathers do sometimes. When I finally let him go I could see the tears streaming down his face, even in the pouring rain. I remember thinking, "Why is it so easy for men to cry in the rain?" And I felt my own tears mixing with the water from the heavens. As Roland walked into his building, I hoped he would feel better knowing someone cared enough to come out in a storm looking for him, that someone loved him enough to embarrass him on the street by that love.